MW01107691

Spring
Wildflowers

*Albert E. Roland
and A. Randall Olson*

Nimbus Publishing &
The Nova Scotia Museum
Halifax, Nova Scotia, 1993

© Crown copyright, Province of Nova Scotia, 1993

93 94 95 96 97 98 99 7 6 5 4 3 2 1

Produced as part of the Nova Scotia Museum
Program of the Department of Education, Province
of Nova Scotia

Minister: Honourable John D. MacEachern
Deputy Minister: Armand F. Pinard

A product of the Nova Scotia Government
Co-publishing Program

Illustrated by: Albert E. Roland, A. Randall Olson
and Elizabeth Owen
Design by: Jay Rutherford
Printed by: McCurdy Printing & Typesetting Limited
Produced by the Department of Supply and Services
and the Nova Scotia Museum

Canadian Cataloguing in Publication Data
Olson, Arthur Randall, 1952-

Spring Wildflowers

(Field Guide Series)
Co-published by the Nova Scotia Museum.

ISBN 1-55109-050-3

1. Wildflowers—Nova Scotia—Identification.
2. Wildflowers—Nova Scotia—Pictorial Works.
I. Roland, A. E. (Albert Edward). 1910-1991 II. Owen,
Elizabeth. III. Nova Scotia Museum. IV. Title. V. Series:
Field guide series. (Halifax, N.S.)

QK203.N6057 1993   582.13'09716   C93-098579-6

*Cover photo by Alex Wilson depicting Blue Flag
(Iris versicolor) found throughout Nova Scotia in late
spring.*

For Ella, Vicki,
and all who are winter-weary

Those of us who live in Atlantic Canada and upper New England know that the price we pay for our long, warm autumns is all too often a cold and difficult spring. However, the season's first flowers are always a welcome sign for winter-weary people, bringing a sense of relief and excitement with the promise of nature renewed.

This book was written to help you identify most flowering trees, shrubs, and plants that bloom in our region during the spring. Our goal is to provide a relatively "user-friendly" field manual designed specifically for the non-scientist interested in identifying only the spring flowers of our region. We caution users, however, that you will eventually be confronted with scientific names. Although common names are more manageable, their exclusive use is fraught with dangers. For example, a flower's common name may not be the same from county to county nor province to province. There are many examples where one common name is used for more than one type of flower. There are even flowers that do not have common names. In any case, we hope that as you use this book you will become familiar with both common and scientific names.

The drawings in this book are meant to show the general form or appearance of the flowering plants. They represent a true collaborative effort; the authors produced draft drawings, sometimes even sharing the work on a single drawing, so that one illustrated the leaves and stems while the other added the flowers and certain other details. The unity of artistic style is the contribution of Elizabeth Owen. We hope that our efforts in this respect will enable visual comparisons in the field to result in successful identification of the flower.

Nova Scotia is relatively rich and varied in flowering trees, shrubs, and plants, which can make "botanizing" in the spring exceptionally rewarding. We encourage you to pursue in-depth investigations using more comprehensive works. Enjoy!

Acknowledgements

We are very grateful to the Department of Biology, Nova Scotia Agricultural College, for the use of their facilities, especially for the unrestricted access to the reference collection of the A. E. Roland Herbarium. Our many friends and colleagues provided the support and encouragement necessary to see the project to completion.

Certain individuals associated with the Nova Scotia Museum deserve special comment. John Hennigar–Shuh and Etta Moffatt from the Museum's Publications Committee were instrumental in the development and promotion of the concept of this book. Barbara Robertson was our manuscript editor; her critical eye, fresh approach, and professionalism have resulted in a better, more usable book. Although demanding as an editor, she always seemed to inject the appropriate amount of enthusiasm and humour into the process of revising the manuscript.

Four other professionals also contributed greatly to the polish of the book you have in your hands. Elizabeth Owen, our illustrator, breathed life into our often "flat" drawings, with the guidance and support of Alex Wilson, the botanist at the Nova Scotia Museum of Natural History. Susan Lucy, from the Department of Supply and Services, did the final copy edit and worked on the index. Then Jay Rutherford, our designer, took all the pieces and made them work wonderfully together.

Finally, we are indebted to Dianne Stevens of the Department of Biology, Nova Scotia Agricultural College, for her tireless efforts and enthusiasm during virtually every stage of the manuscript preparation. Ms. Stevens served as proof reader, a sounding board for our ideas, and a critic. In addition to organizing the index, she made several valuable suggestions for changing the text and modifying the illustrations in order to better meet the objective of this book. Thank you, Dianne.

Note from the author

Dr. Albert E. Roland, Professor Emeritus of Biology at the Nova Scotia Agricultural College, passed away on September 17, 1991, at his home in Truro. Dr. Roland and I finished the initial draft of this book shortly before he became ill. He was unable to participate fully in the necessary revisions which followed; therefore, I assume full responsibility for any errors or omissions.

Dr. A. Randall Olson
Truro, Nova Scotia
April 1992

Contents

The **Table of Contents** that is found just before this section is your key to identifying spring-flowering plants.

Unlike traditional botanical keys, this one is easy to use. With its help, you'll be able to identify a spring wildflower simply by looking carefully at both the flower and the plant it comes from and asking yourself a few basic questions.

The process is very straightforward. The Table of Contents will tell you what questions to ask and what order to ask them in.

Here's what you'll need to know to ask and answer these questions.

1. When did you find your flower?

We have organized the plants in this book in three sections according to their approximate flowering times:

Early Spring = April
Mid-Spring = May
Late Spring = the first half of June

Of course, these are only rough divisions; geographical location and local environmental conditions have a big influence on when plants flower. There will always be some overlap between the end of one section and the beginning of the next. So, if you are unable to identify a flower using the choices in one section try those presented in the next.

2. What sort of plant does your flower come from?

Is it woody or non-woody?
One of the most obvious ways of separating plants is to group them as being either **woody** or **non-woody**. We use that distinction in this book.

The stem of a **woody** plant will eventually become thick, rigid, and covered with some form of bark. In contrast, the stem of a **non-woody** (herbaceous) plant usually remains green and supple throughout the plant's life. The violets are good examples of non-woody (herbaceous) plants. Trees and shrubs are good examples of woody plants.

Be Careful! Certain trailing (creeping or sprawling) woody plants may appear to be non-woody, but this appearance can be deceptive. When you look carefully, the lowest portion of the main stem may turn out to be woody.

Is your plant a "monocot" or a "dicot"?
Flowering plants are divided into the **monocots** and **dicots**. These terms come from Latin words which refer to the number of embryonic leaves a plant has.

Relax, we know that such features are often difficult to examine outside a laboratory. Fortunately, monocots and dicots also have characteristics that are relatively easy to observe while examining the plant in the field.

Monocots usually have flower parts arranged in sets of three. For example, a typical monocot flower may have three sepals and three petals. Also, the major veins in the leaves of monocots may appear to be parallel to each other. The Common Blue-eyed Grass is an example of a monocot.

Dicots, in contrast, usually have flower parts arranged in sets of four or five. In addition, the major veins in dicot leaves have an overall net-like appearance. A rose is an example of a dicot.

As with all generalizations, there are exceptions; but these are not serious enough to concern us here.

3. What sort of flower does your plant have?

Is your flower complete or reduced?
Most people have a general idea of what makes a flower a flower. When they think of a flower they most often conjure up an image of a "showy" structure with **sepals** and **petals** and both male parts (**stamens**) and female parts (**carpels**)—a complete flower.

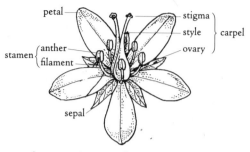

In nature, however, it is not always easy to recognize flowers as flowers. In addition to the wide variety of colours and shapes, certain flowers do not have all of the parts we generally expect to find. Such **reduced** flowers may also be very small and have only some of the parts found in a **complete** flower.

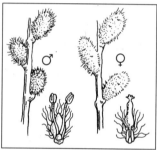

Catkins, for example, are collections of either male flowers or female flowers and have no petals. Pussy-willows, which are eagerly collected in the spring by children and adults alike, are **male catkins**. So, in other words, the tiny individual flowers that make up Pussy-willows are all male and do not have any petals or female parts. The female catkins appear later.

Are the flowers regular or irregular?
If the petals are similar to one another and they radiate from a central point, the flower is said to be **regular**. The buttercups are examples of regular flowers.

If some of the petals are different from one another and the blossom does not have a radial appearance, the flower is said to be **irregular**. The violets are examples of irregular flowers.

4. What other special characteristics does your plant or flower have?

We have also grouped plants by other special features such as prickles, spines or thorns, when this has been useful.

Similarly, we have also grouped flowers by colour.

Here's how it works!

An Example

During a walk through a hardwood stand in Cumberland County on May 20th you find a plant with a small white flower that looks like this.

- Because the date is May 20th, look under the **Mid-Spring** section of the Table of Contents.

- There's nothing woody about this plant, so go to the **Non-Woody (Herbaceous) Plants** listings in the Mid-Spring section.

- Because this flower has four petals and net-like veins in its leaves, you proceed to the **Dicots** listings under the Non-woody heading.

- Because the petals of the flower are similar to one another and radiate from a central point, go next to the **Regular flowers** listings under the Dicots heading.

- Finally, because your flower is white, the Table of Contents directs you to page **5 0.** A collection of drawings and descriptions for 19 plants that are non-woody dicots with regular white flowers begins on that page.

- When you compare your flower with the drawings in that section, you find that it matches one of the illustrations on page **5 3.**

- Congratulations! It turns out that you have a **Toothwort.**

Some Useful Terms

Alluvial – soil typically associated with flood plains.

Alternate – arranged first on one side and then on the other at different levels or points along an axial line, not side by side

Annual – completes its life cycle in one growing season.

Anther – a pouch or sac-like structure that produces pollen. *(See illustration below.)*

Apex – the tip, get the point?

Axil – the angle between the upper side of the leaf stalk and the stem. *(See illustration of a Compound leaf with leaflets, p. XIV)*

Basal – located near the base.

Biennial – completes its life cycle in two growing seasons.

Bisexual flower – a flower with both male parts (**stamens**) and female parts (**carpels**). *(See illustration below.)*

Blade – the flat or expanded portion of a leaf or leaflet. *(See illustration of a Compound leaf with leaflets, p. XIV)*

Bract – a small, leaf-like structure. Bracts may vary in size, form and colour. *(See illustrations of Trembling Aspen, p. 3, and Pussy-willow, p. 4)*

Bud scale – a small bract associated with a bud. *(See illustration of a Compound leaf with leaflets, p. XIV)*

Calyx – an inclusive name for all the **sepals**.

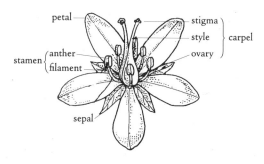

Typical flower structure

Calyx-lobe – the rounded tip of a sepal. *(See illustration of American Elm, p. 6)*

Cane – a stem with a hollow or spongy centre.

Capsule – a type of dry fruit containing many seeds. *(See illustration of Cottony-headed Willow, p. 20)*

Carpel – the basic unit of the female part of a flower, usually consisting of a **stigma**, a **style**, and an **ovary**. *(See illustration of* **Typical flower** *structure, previous page.)*

Carpellate – having to do with **carpels** or female parts of flowers, so, carpellate flowers = female flowers.

Catkin – an elongated cluster of small male or female flowers without petals, resembling a cat's tail. Male catkins and female catkins may occur either on the same individual plant or on separate individual plants. *(See illustrations of Balsam Poplar, p. 2, and Pussy-willow, p. 4)*

Ciliate – having a fringe of hairs. *(See illustration of Twisted-stalk, p. 101.)*

Cleistogamous – a condition in which flower buds remain closed resulting in self-pollination.

Common – frequently observed; occurs frequently over a large (broad) geographical area.

Compound leaf – a single leaf composed of leaflets.

(See illustration on next page.)

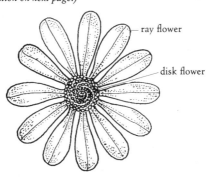

ray flower

disk flower

Composite Head

Coniferous – having to do with cone-bearing trees.

Corolla – an inclusive name for all the **petals**.

Deciduous – refers to trees that shed their leaves each fall.

Disk flower – small, stalkless flowers that make up the central portion of a composite head. *(See illustration of Composite Head, p. XIII.)*

Escape – a commonly cultivated plant that has run wild or has sprung up from self-sown seeds.

Hybrid – usually refers to the offspring of two different species.

Inflorescence – a general term referring to an aggregation or arrangement of flowers.

Intervale – low-lying area of rich land between hills or by a river.

Lanceolate – usually refers to a leaf (but it could refer to a stem or other part of a plant) that is longer than it is wide and tapers to a lance-shaped tip. *(See illustration of Lance-leaved Violet, p. 48.)*

Leaflet – a single division of a compound leaf. *(See illustration below.)*

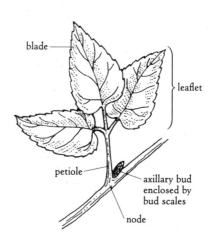

Compound leaf with three leaflets

Leaf stalk (petiole) – structure that attaches the leaf blade to the stem. *(See illustration of a Compound leaf with leaflets, p. XIV.)*

Local – having to do with a particular place.

Midrib – the centre or main vein of a leaf.

Node – place on the stem where the leaves are attached. *(See illustration of a Compound leaf with leaflets, p. XIV.)*

Ovary – the part of the carpel that contains the seeds. *(See Typical flower structure, p. XII.)*

Palmate – refers to structures radiating outward from a common centre. *(See illustration of Black Snakeroot, p. 117.)*

Perfect flower – a single flower that has both male and female parts. *(See illustration of Typical flower structure, p. XII.)*

Petal – one of the, usually coloured, components of a flower. *(See illustration of Typical flower structure, p. XII.)*

Prickle – a small, sharp outgrowth from the surface, usually from a stem, of a plant. *(See illustration of Bristly Black Currant, p. 30.)*

Raceme – a cluster of *stalked* flowers with an elongated, unbranched central axis (compare with **spike**, below). *(See illustration of Common Barberry, p. 29.)*

Ray flower – small, stalkless flowers with elongated **corollas,** which make up the periphery of a composite head. *(Compare with **Disk flower** above. See Composite Head illustration, p. XIII.)*

Runner – a small, slender, horizontal stem that usually grows out from the main stem, along the surface of the ground. *(See illustration of Woodland Strawberry, p. 54.)*

Scattered – dispersed here and there, but not everywhere.

Sepal – one of the outer, usually green, components of a flower. *(See illustration of Typical flower structure, p. XII.)*

Spike – a cluster of *stalkless* flowers on an elongated, unbranched central axis (compare with **Raceme** above). *(See illustration of Narrow-leaved Plantain, p. 116.)*

Spine – a hard, sharp, pointed structure, a modified leaf. *(See illustration of Gooseberry, p. 30.)*

Stamen – the basic unit of the male part of a flower, usually consisting of an **anther** attached to a filament. *(See illustration of Typical flower structure, p. XII.)*

Staminate – having to do with **stamens** or the male parts of flowers, so, staminate flowers = male flowers.

Stigma – the part of the **carpel** that receives pollen. *(See illustration of Typical flower structure, p. XII.)*

Stolon – another name for a slender, horizontal stem *(see **runner**, above)*.

Style – the narrowed extension of the carpel that supports the **stigma**. *(See illustration of Typical flower structure, p. XII.)*

Subtending – situated directly beneath.

Talus – a sloping mass of rocky fragments lying at the base of a cliff.

Tap-root – the relatively large, main root.

Tendril – a thin, string-like organ used by climbing plants such as certain vines; may be a modified leaf or stem. *(See illustration of Tufted Vetch, p. 107.)*

Thorn – a branch modified as a pointed, sharp projection. *(See illustration of Hawthorn, Crataegus chrysocarpa, p. 31.)*

Umbel – a cluster of flowers in which the stalks arise from a common point; a flat-topped **inflorescence**. *(See illustration of Wild Chervil, p. 109.)*

Unisexual flower – having only male or only female parts in an individual flower. *(See illustration of Broom Crowberry, p. 7.)*

Variable – not always exactly the same.

Whorl – a circular arrangement of leaves or flower parts around a central stalk. *(See illustration of Purple Trillium, p. 43.)*

Woody Plants

FLOWERS IN CATKINS

A Word about Catkins

Depending on the kind of plant, male catkins and female catkins may or may not look similar, and may or may not occur on the same individual plant.

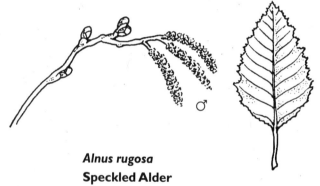

Alnus rugosa
Speckled Alder

The Speckled Alder flowers early, forming long male catkins before the end of April. The female catkins are very small; they emerge from their buds in the fall and overwinter outside the bud. When mature, they form a hard, egg-shaped cone about 1 cm long, which may last for a season or two. Speckled Alder is found on low ground throughout the province.

A Word about Poplars

The poplars appear soon after the willows and their fluffy bunches of seeds form late in April or early May. The catkins are much longer and more slender than those of the willows.

Populus alba
White or Silver-leaved Poplar

The young twigs of these poplars and the undersides of the leaves are cotton-woolly. Older trees have oval leaves, while more recent plantings often have deeply lobed leaves, and go by the name of Silver Maple. You will find these occasionally as large trees around dwellings or along roadsides.

Populus balsamifera
Balsam Poplar

The buds of Balsam Poplar are large and very sticky, and the trees are conspicuous in early spring because the dark green of their foliage shows up against the lighter foliage of neighbouring trees. In central Nova Scotia the Balsam Poplar is found only along streams and on intervales, but it becomes much more common as you move eastward, and it is widespread in Cape Breton.

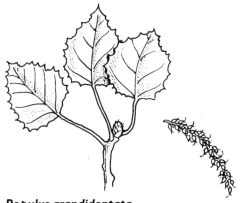

Populus grandidentata
Large-toothed Poplar

The Large-toothed Poplar is best identified, even in winter, by its finely hairy buds. The leaves, when they appear, are much more coarsely toothed than those of the other species. It is common throughout the province.

Populus tremuloides
Trembling Aspen

This poplar is best identified by its smooth and shiny buds. Note that these buds have several scales and that the bracts on the catkins are finely lobed or divided. It is common throughout the province.

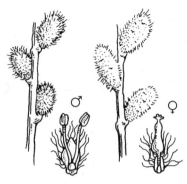

Salix discolor
Pussy-willow

The earliest of our willows, the Pussy-willow is looked for as an early sign of spring. Like all willows, it has its male and female catkins on separate bushes. The twigs are smooth, and the catkins appear before the leaves begin to unfold. The bracts of the catkins are black, and the one basal bud scale, as is typical of all willows, is at the bottom. It is common throughout Nova Scotia.

Salix humilis
Small Pussy-willow

This is much like the other Pussy-willow, *Salix discolor*, except that the twigs are covered with fine hairs. The stamens, when they first appear, tend to be reddish. It is common throughout Nova Scotia.

Salix purpurea
Purple Osier,
Basket Willow

Purple Osier is a large shrub or small tree with slender branches. The slender, 3 cm long catkins form in late April before the leaves begin to appear. The tips of the bracts are black. This tree was formerly planted as an ornamental and is common in many towns in southwestern Nova Scotia; it is rare in the country.

Woody Plants

FLOWERS NOT IN CATKINS

Trees

Acer rubrum
Red Maple

The Red Maple's tiny red to yellowish flowers cover mature trees early in the spring well before the leaves are out. Note that all maples have their buds and leaves at a node and opposite each other on the stem. These trees are common throughout the province.

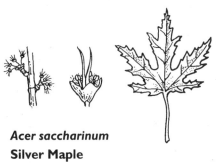

Acer saccharinum
Silver Maple

The Silver Maple is a tall, graceful tree. Like the Red Maple, its flowers appear before its leaves. Its young fruits are whitish-woolly, while those of the Red Maple are smooth. The Silver Maple is not a common tree here, although it is occasionally planted as an ornamental; it is native along the St. John River in New Brunswick.

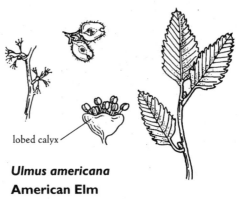

lobed calyx

Ulmus americana
American Elm

Tufts of small greenish flowers appear on the American Elm in early spring before the leaves. These flowers have four to nine calyx-lobes but no petals. Small oval fruits appear with the leaves but drop off soon after. Elms can be identified later by the shape of the leaves; typically, the two sides of the leaf are uneven at the base. American Elms are scattered throughout the central and northern regions of the province, on the intervales and along river valleys.

Ulmus glabra
Scotch Elm

This is an introduced tree much like the American Elm in most respects, including the flowers. The fruits, which also develop before the leaves, are much larger than those of the American Elm (over 2 cm long). These trees are associated with established communities and older dwelling sites.

Woody Plants

FLOWERS NOT IN CATKINS

Low shrubs

Corema conradii
Broom Crowberry

This plant is low and bushy, perhaps to 30 cm tall, and has narrow, needle-like evergreen leaves. It flowers about the end of April or the beginning of May, with tiny clusters of stamens or carpels at the tips of the branches. The flowers, both male and female, have no petals and thus are not at all showy. Found on sandy or rocky soils, it is common in the Annapolis Valley and scattered from Yarmouth and Shelburne counties to Guysborough County.

Daphne mezereum
Daphne

Daphne is a shrub several metres high, whose branches are covered with rose or pale pink flowers at the end of April or in early May. These flowers have petals and (take a closer look) eight stamens, like the flowers of Shepherdia. The berries are red; the seed in them is deadly poisonous. Daphne is found near old French locations, but is becoming rarer.

fruit

Lonicera canadensis
American Fly-honeysuckle

The American Fly-honeysuckle flowers in early spring. The leaves and buds are opposite on the twigs; the hanging pairs of creamy-yellow flowers are conspicuous as the leaves unfold. It is scattered through mixed and deciduous forests, especially in the northern part of the province.

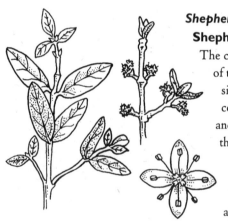

Shepherdia canadensis
Shepherdia

The conspicuous feature of this shrub is the silvery-brown, scaly covering on the twigs and the undersides of the leaves. The small, brownish flowers crowded near the tips of the twigs, appear before the leaf-buds open. This bush, about a metre tall, is found around gypsum outcrops or, very rarely, scattered elsewhere in alkaline soils from Brier Island to northern Cape Breton.

Viburnum alnifolium
Hobblebush

This tall shrub is also one of the first to flower at the end of April or early in May. It is conspicuous since the flowers occur in large clusters with the outer circle large and white. The twigs and branches of the flower cluster are covered with tiny brown scales. Hobblebush is found in rich hardwoods and shaded ravines. It is rare in southwestern Nova Scotia, but is becoming common in northern Cape Breton.

Trailing and/or Non-Woody (Herbaceous) Plants

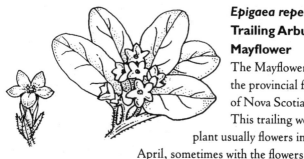

Epigaea repens
Trailing Arbutus, Mayflower

The Mayflower is the provincial flower of Nova Scotia. This trailing woody plant usually flowers in April, sometimes with the flowers partially buried in the grass and old leaves. The fragrant flowers vary from white to pink to an occasional deep rose colour. This common plant is found in pastures and barrens throughout Nova Scotia on acidic, well-drained soils.

Hepatica americana
Hepatica

The three-lobed leaves of the Hepatica are distinctive. They survive over winter and new ones are formed after the plant flowers. The flowers are light blue, with 5 to 10 petal-like sepals but no petals. The plant is 10–15 cm tall and very rare. In the past, it has been found in several locations in dryish woods in Central Nova Scotia, but few places are now known for it.

Sanguinaria canadensis
Blood-root

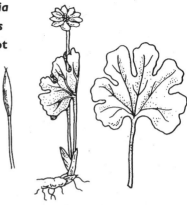

Blood-root plants grow together in groups and are anywhere from 4 to 15 cm tall. The flowers are borne one to a stalk, surrounded by an unfolding leaf. The flowers are nearly white, with eight or more petals, which fall very quickly. The stout rootstocks have a bright orange-red juice, which stains any broken part of the stem or leaves and has also been used to produce a red dye. Blood-root grows on low ground on rich intervales in Kings and Hants counties.

Symplocarpus foetidus
Skunk Cabbage

hood

The spike of flowers, surrounded by the greenish-yellow hood, is produced about the end of April or the first of May. The large leaves, somewhat like those of rhubarb, appear later. The early plants are only about 10 cm tall. Skunk Cabbage gets its name from the strong, unpleasant smell it gives off when its leaves and stalk are crushed. This plant is found only in southern Digby and Yarmouth counties in wet thickets, along brooks, and in mossy woods.

Tussilago farfara
Coltsfoot

Coltsfoot grows in beds of dandelion-like, yellow flowers, but
with numerous very narrow rays and bracts upon the stem. In
summer, Coltsfoot has broad leaves that are finely woolly
beneath. It is an introduced plant, sometimes called "Son before
the Father" because its flowers appear before its leaves. Common
in gravelly soil, it spreads actively by running rootstocks.

Woody Plants

FLOWERS IN CATKINS

Trees

A Word about Catkins

Depending on the kind of plant, male catkins and female catkins may or may not look similar, and may or may not occur on the same individual plant.

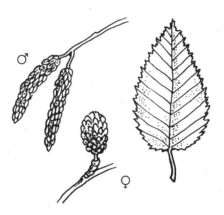

Betula alleghaniensis
Yellow Birch

Except for young trees, or for old trees with very rough bark, the yellowish papery bark will identify this tree. For young bushes, note that the leaves have 9 to 11 pairs of main veins, while other birches have fewer. Another feature is the oval shape of the female catkins. The twigs of the Yellow Birch also have a wintergreen taste. It is found throughout Nova Scotia, but is most common in the mixed forests in the eastern part of the province.

Betula cordifolia
Heart-leaved Birch

The Heart-leaved Birch is very similar to the White Birch, but now it is being recognized as a separate species. The bark is a more creamy white, and the leaves are prominently heart-shaped at their bases. It is scattered, especially near the coast along the Bay of Fundy and eastward to Cape Breton.

Betula papyrifera
White or
Paper Birch

This tree is best identified by its white, papery bark. The leaves are wedge-shaped at the base and the male catkins are in twos or threes at the ends of the branches. White Birch is common throughout Nova Scotia and occasionally forms pure stands after a fire.

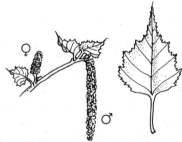

Betula populifolia
Wire or Gray Birch

This is a slender wiry birch with the bark a more ashy white and not forming layers as in the White Birch. The leaves are almost triangular with long pointed tips. Early in the season Wire Birch has male catkins borne singly, instead of in groups. This pasture tree, or large shrub, is common from Yarmouth County to Antigonish County, but is very rare in Cape Breton.

Ostrya virginiana
Hop-hornbeam

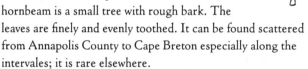

The male catkins on this tree
become longer during
May, while the tiny
female ones grow out of
the bud as the leaves
unfold later. The Hop-
hornbeam is a small tree with rough bark. The
leaves are finely and evenly toothed. It can be found scattered
from Annapolis County to Cape Breton especially along the
intervales; it is rare elsewhere.

Quercus borealis
Red Oak

Red Oak catkins appear late in
May and are present in
early June as the young
leaves unfold. The male
catkins are long and
slender; the female ones
consist of pairs of carpels
in the leaf axils at the tips of
the twigs. The Red Oak is
found throughout Nova Scotia to northern Cape Breton, but is
only scattered here and there on the sandy soil of the Annapolis
Valley and on the granitic areas in the southern part of the
province.

Quercus robur
English Oak

This is a smaller and more compact tree than the Red Oak, but as in the Red Oak, the yellowish-green flowers appear as catkins. The rounded lobes on the leaves help to identify English Oak. Later in the year, its acorns, which are much longer than Red Oak acorns, provide a means of identification. You can find the English Oak scattered as an escape or as a roadside tree from Annapolis to Halifax and Truro.

Salix alba
White or French Willow

This is our most common tree-willow. Both the male and female catkins and the leaves are rather long and narrow. It was formerly planted as an ornamental but is now found in many habitats throughout Nova Scotia. Many of our roadside trees are hybrids with other willow species; it frequently escapes and vigorous young bushes may often be seen.

Woody Plants

FLOWERS IN CATKINS

Shrubs

Alnus crispa
Downy Alder

The Downy Alder is a later flowering species than the Speckled Alder (*see* p. 1). The Downy Alder's male catkins appear with the leaves, and its female catkins grow out of the bud. Look for these tiny female catkins on the new growth; they last for at least a season and look like tiny pine cones in their second year. This alder is common throughout Nova Scotia, especially near the coast and on drier soils.

Comptonia peregrina
Sweet Fern

This is an aromatic low shrub that grows 30 to 80 cm tall. The male catkins are numerous and grow on the ends of the twigs. They are conspicuous during April and mature during the middle of May. The smaller, less conspicuous female catkins may or may not be on the same twigs as the male catkins. The leaves, which are long and narrow, are deeply lobed along the sides. Crush the leaves to discover their distinctive aroma, which some people compare to that of creosote. It grows commonly on light soils in mainland Nova Scotia and is common in blueberry fields, but is absent in Cape Breton.

Corylus cornuta
Hazelnut

A low slender shrub, Hazelnut is distinguished from similar species by having double-toothed leaves, that is, leaves with small teeth on the larger teeth. The male catkins lengthen during early May. The female flowers are visible only as tufts of bright red stigmas growing out of a bud. The slender twigs and the grayish color of the Hazelnut's bark also help to identify it. Found generally in dry and open woods it is often abundant as an understory shrub.

Myrica gale
Sweet Gale

This wiry shrub,
1-2 m tall, bears
male catkins that
are conspicuous in
early May, while the
female ones, which
are small and cone-like, may be found along the young branches.
The undersides of the leaves are covered with resinous dots.
Sweet Gale is common throughout Nova Scotia at the edge of
ponds, along still waters, and in boggy land.

Myrica pensylvanica
Bayberry

This stout branching
shrub is 1-2 m tall.
The catkins appear
in late May or early
June with a number
of leaves formed
above them on the
stem. Male and female
catkins are usually produced on
separate plants. As with Sweet Gale, Bayberry leaves are
prominently dotted with resin on their undersides. Bayberry's
aroma is a pleasant feature of coastal barrens. It is found
throughout Nova Scotia and is particularly common in the
southwestern part of the province, growing on drier land than
Sweet Gale.

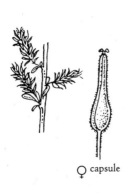
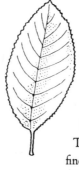

♀ capsule

Salix bebbiana
Beaked Willow

The Beaked Willow catkins (male) appear with the leaves and their bracts lend them a light yellowish-brown hue. The capsules (female) are finely hairy and become long-stalked as they develop. These may remain on the bushes for some time after flowering. Beaked Willow is our most common willow, found in many habitats throughout the province.

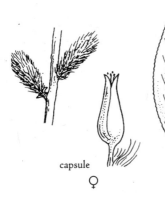

capsule

♀

Salix eriocephala
Cottony-headed Willow

This willow is rather variable in both size and leaf shape, growing from small bushes to large shrubs. The leaves are usually narrow but occasionally much wider and heart-shaped at the base. The capsules are smooth, reddish-green, and abundant. It is common along every stream and river in central and eastern Nova Scotia.

Salix lucida
Shining Willow

The best aid in identifying this willow is its large shiny leaf with a long pointed tip. The male catkins have five or more stamens to each bract. Although scattered throughout the province, Shining Willow is usually found on sand bars along rivers, but occasionally it may grow in wet ground, such as along ditches. It is a larger shrub than most other willows.

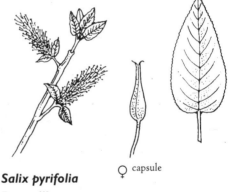

♀ capsule

Salix pyrifolia
Bog-willow

This willow is typical of the very wet ground of bogs. In spring, the twigs and young leaves have a distinctive salmon colour. The catkins are present in late May or early June, as the leaves enlarge, and the smooth capsules of the female catkins and the pale-green undersides of the leaves are conspicuous. It is common throughout most of Nova Scotia but is rare near the Atlantic coast.

Woody Plants

FLOWERS NOT IN CATKINS

Trees

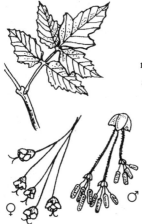

Acer negundo
Manitoba Maple, Box Elder
The Manitoba Maple is our only maple with leaves divided into separate leaflets. The flowers are small, without petals; they appear with the leaves and are of two kinds, male and female. Manitoba Maple is frequently found near well-established communities and along roadsides throughout the province.

Acer pensylvanicum
Striped Maple
The Striped Maple flowers from late May to early June, with the flowers in hanging racemes. Note the three-lobed leaves with their fine toothing. Widespread but rarely abundant, it is common in southwestern Nova Scotia but absent in northern Cape Breton.

Acer platanoides
Norway Maple

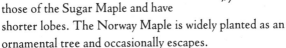

The Norway Maple flowers, which are larger and showier than those of the other maples, appear with the young leaves and are borne upright at the ends of the twigs. The leaves are more square in outline than those of the Sugar Maple and have shorter lobes. The Norway Maple is widely planted as an ornamental tree and occasionally escapes.

Acer saccharum
Sugar Maple

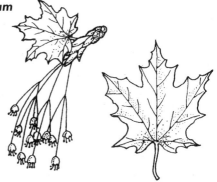

Sugar Maples flower in early May as the leaves begin to unfold. The flowers occur in tufts, are very small with no petals, and are either male or female. They grow on slender stalks and are quite different from the maple flowers that appear in April. Note the slender ends of the main lobes of these leaves. Sugar Maples are found throughout Nova Scotia.

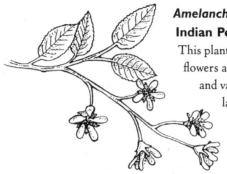

Amelanchier laevis
Indian Pear, Shadbush

This plant is quite variable; it flowers and fruits abundantly and varies in size from large trees down to low shrubs. Its bronze foliage is conspicuous in spring, before flowering. All the species of *Amelanchier* are recognizable when they are in flower because their petals are several times longer than they are wide. The Indian Pear is the most common species in western Nova Scotia, where entire hillsides are white with it in May.

Amelanchier wiegandii
Bilberry

This is much like the Indian Pear but its clusters of flowers are more compact, and the white flowers themselves have shorter petals. It is often considered to be a mixture of hybrids and may grow into a large tree. Upon close examination, Bilberry's main distinguishing features are the woolly top of the ovary and the hairy lower surface of the unfolding leaves. This species is common throughout the province.

Fagus grandifolia
Beech

Beech trees may produce flowers that go unnoticed. Basically, the flowers consist only of the essential male and female parts. The tiny clusters of stamens can be seen near the end of May, and the female flowers, which produce the beechnuts, can be seen all during June. The smooth gray bark is typical. Later, the veining of the leaves, with each vein ending in a tooth on the margin, will identify the tree. Beech trees are most commonly found growing in the mixed hardwood regions of the province.

Prunus pensylvanica
Pin Cherry

Pin Cherry flowers appear during mid-May and are in small white clusters. The leaves are much narrower than those of the other cherries. Pin Cherry is common in barrens, burned-over areas, and open woods.

Pyrus malus
Apple

Apple trees flower from late May to early June. The white to pinkish flowers are the most showy of this group of plants. It is widely found, with common escapes wherever apples are grown.

Sorbus americana
Mountain Ash

The Mountain Ash is a small tree that produces large flat clusters of creamy white flowers in early June. The leaves are large with a number of leaflets, which are long and tapering on the ends. The leaves, stems, and particularly the buds are smooth. The Mountain Ash is a native tree and occurs frequently from Yarmouth to Cape Breton.

Sorbus aucuparia
Rowan Tree

The Rowan Tree is much like the Mountain Ash but has smaller and blunter leaves. The two species can be distinguished by their buds; Mountain Ash has smooth shiny buds while the Rowan Tree has woolly buds. This is an introduced species, which is commonly planted and occasionally escapes.

Woody Plants

FLOWERS NOT IN CATKINS

Low shrubs with spines or prickles

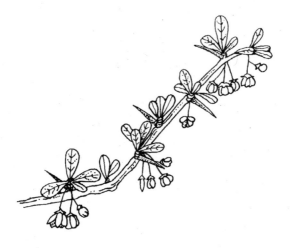

Berberis thunbergii
Japanese Barberry

The Japanese Barberry is a small, thorny bush with greenish flowers about 8 mm wide in small clusters. The leaves and flowers are in the axils of single thorns. Commonly planted as an ornamental, it is sometimes found as an escape.

Berberis vulgaris
Common Barberry

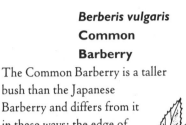

The Common Barberry is a taller bush than the Japanese Barberry and differs from it in these ways: the edge of the leaves are bristly-toothed, it generally has three spines at a node, and the flower clusters are in hanging racemes. Ironically, the Common Barberry is quite rare in Nova Scotia, occurring only occasionally as an escape.

Ribes glandulosum
Skunk Currant

The Skunk Currant is usually 30 to 50 cm tall and grows in alluvial soil or in mixed woods. It flowers from mid-May to early June. The yellowish-green flowers and the fruit are bristly and, like those of the Bristly Black Currant (*see p.30*), have tiny glands that secrete a sticky substance. The bruised shrub and berries have a strong odour, but the berries are juicy and quite tasty, although rarely numerous. The Skunk Currant is also characterized by an absence of spines and is our most common wild currant, common to abundant throughout Nova Scotia.

Ribes hirtellum
Gooseberry

Gooseberry flowers appear in late May, are 4–7 mm long, yellowish-green, and occur in clusters of one to five. The number of spines along the stem may vary from plant to plant. The leaves are deeply divided into three to five lobes. The Gooseberry is usually present but never common; you can find it throughout Nova Scotia along stone walls and in rocky woods and pastures.

Ribes lacustre
Bristly Black Currant

The flowers of Bristly Black Currant occur in drooping racemes and appear in late May or early June. The yellowish-green flowers and the fruit have tiny glands that secrete a sticky substance; and the stem is finely bristly. This plant is easy to recognize because its leaves are more deeply divided than those of the Gooseberry. Bristly Black Currant is found throughout Nova Scotia in rocky woods and ravines. North of a line from Annapolis to Guysborough, it is found in the hardwood forest.

Woody Plants

FLOWERS NOT IN CATKINS

Large shrubs with stout thorns

A word about Hawthorns

Hawthorns are common tall bushes with abundant showy white flowers. A number of species occur in Nova Scotia, and the differences between them are often very subtle, so don't be discouraged if you have problems telling them apart.

Crataegus chrysocarpa Hawthorn

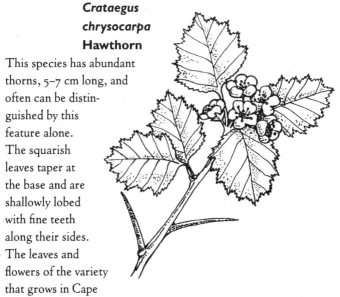

This species has abundant thorns, 5–7 cm long, and often can be distinguished by this feature alone. The squarish leaves taper at the base and are shallowly lobed with fine teeth along their sides. The leaves and flowers of the variety that grows in Cape Breton tend to be somewhat woolly, while in the mainland variety, they are smooth. This Hawthorn is found throughout the province and is probably our most common type.

Crataegus grayana
Hawthorn

This Hawthorn closely resembles the preceding species, but it has smaller leaves and about 20 pink stamens. It is common throughoutthe province, but especially so in northern Cape Breton.

Crataegus macracantha
Hawthorn

The main distinguishing feature of this quite variable species is the deeply lobed or cut sepals, which are often glandular and more easily observed at the flower bud stage. The anthers of the stamens are reddish. This Hawthorn is especially common in northern Cape Breton, common in eastern Nova Scotia, and occasionally scattered west to Digby County and Cumberland County.

Crataegus macrosperma Hawthorn

This is a species of Hawthorn with leaves that are wide, and often pointed at the tip with shallow lobes. The leaf blade is thinner than those of the previous species. The flower cluster may be smooth or lightly hairy. There are usually five to eight stamens, and they are usually yellow; red stamens indicate a hybrid with another introduced species. The tall bushes usually grow singly and are scattered along roadsides, in pastures, and at the edge of lakes.

Crataegus monogyna English Hawthorn

The white-flowered English Hawthorn is the earliest species to bloom and is the only one with short stubby thorns and deeply lobed leaves. The English Hawthorn is widely distributed throughout the province. It is our only introduced species; all the others are native.

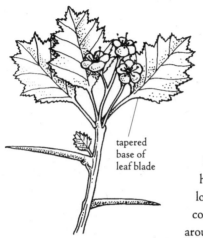

tapered
base of
leaf blade

Crataegus scabrida
Hawthorn

This is a robust type of Hawthorn with stout thorns. It flowers in late May or early June. The leaf blades taper sharply toward the leaf stalks and the blades have numerous sharp lobes. This plant is very common in the valleys around Truro and Pictou, where it often covers consider-able areas. (Some bushes have leaves that are less sharply lobed and more oval in shape; they belong to a variation of this species.)

Crataegus submollis
Hawthorn

This Hawthorn has large, densely hairy leaves and softly hairy flower clusters, making it one of our most distinctive species. It is scattered from Lunenburg to Pictou County, often growing in hedges or at the edge of fields.

Woody Plants

FLOWERS NOT IN CATKINS

Shrubs without spines, prickles, or thorns

Amelanchier bartramiana
**Indian Pear,
Service Berry**

The white flowers of this Indian Pear
occur most commonly in groups of
one to three. The fruit is slightly
oval in shape, and the top of the
ovary is always woolly. This
species is found in cool coniferous
woods and in peaty or boggy areas.
It is scattered in southwestern
Nova Scotia but becoming
common from Cumberland County
to northern Cape Breton.

Amelanchier stolonifera
Dwarf Bilberry

The Dwarf Bilberry is a small bush
with nearly oval leaves and large juicy
berries. The leaves appear with the
white flowers and have blunt or
rounded tips and a whitish wool on
their undersides when they are young.
It is common on the sandy soil in the
centre of the Annapolis Valley and
scattered elsewhere.

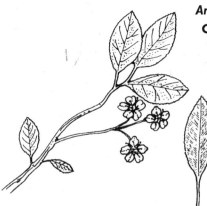

Arctostaphylos uva-ursi
Bearberry

The Bearberry is an evergreen trailing shrub that grows several metres long and may form a solid cover over the ground. The flowers appear in late May or early June and are white, tinged with pink. It is common on the sandy barrens of the Annapolis Valley and occurs elsewhere throughout the province, including northern Cape Breton, as scattered patches in dry areas.

Aronia prunifolia
Chokeberry

This shrub is quite variable in height, growing from 20 cm to 2 m high. The white flowers, which look like small strawberry flowers, appear about the end of May or the first of June. If leaves are present, this plant can be identified by the scattered dark glands along the upper side of the midrib of the leaf blade. It is most common in pastures but found in many habitats from bogs to sandy plains throughout the province.

small brownish scales
on underside of leaf

Chamaedaphne calyculata
Leather-leaf, Cassandra

The white flowers of the Leather-leaf appear in mid-May and are
6–7 mm long. The leaves are evergreen and may appear brownish on their undersides due to numerous tiny scales. These wiry
bushes grow to about a metre tall. They are common throughout
the province at the edges of ponds, bogs, and marshes and
occasionally on poorly drained soils.

Lonicera villosa
Mountain Fly-
honeysuckle

The Mountain Fly-honeysuckle
is a low depressed shrub; its
main distinguishing features
are its opposite buds and oval
leaves. The leaves and young
stems may be densely hairy.
The flowers are cream-
coloured and tend to be clustered
near the ends of the branches. The
berries are edible and of excellent flavour.
This shrub is scattered in boggy land, wet
thickets, and pastures in the northern parts
of the province.

Sambucus pubens
Red-berried Elder

The Red-berried Elder has compound leaves, and large clusters of tiny creamy white or yellow flowers are present in late May or early June. The berries, which mature in late June, are bright red and mildly poisonous. The shrub is common in rocky pastures and hillsides, more or less throughout Nova Scotia.

Non-Woody (Herbaceous) Plants

MONOCOTS

Convallaria majalis
Lily-of-the-valley

These plants are about 15 cm tall and have pure white, bell-like flowers that bloom in late May. Lily-of-the-valley is an ornamental plant that spreads by stout rootstocks and forms patches near houses, in cemeteries, or along roadsides in the southern parts of the province.

Cypripedium arietinum
Ram's-head Lady's-slipper

This orchid is usually in full bloom by the end of May. The blossom characteristically has three separate sepals, two lateral petals, and a lip that usually has a pinkish net-like appearance upon close examination. The Ram's-head Lady's-slipper is associated with those areas of the province that have gypsum-dominated soils.

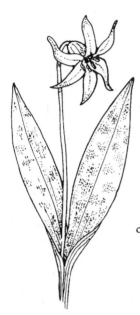

Erythronium americanum
Dog's-tooth Violet, Trout-lily

This plant is about 30 cm tall, with yellow, lily-like flowers. It often spreads in wide beds and can be distinguished from similar plants, such as *Clintonia*, by the dark blotches on its leaves.

The Dog's-tooth Violet is local in eastern Kings County and is common on intervales and in upland woods in central Nova Scotia.

Luzula acuminata
Early Woodrush

This small grass-like plant, less than 30
cm tall, has greenish flowers in an umbel
less than 10 mm wide at the top of the
unbranched stem. The flowers appear in
early May to June. Like all the monocots,
except for the trilliums, the Early
Woodrushes have parallel-veined leaves.
This plant has long hairs on the leaves and the
nodes of the stems. Early Woodrush is
common throughout Nova Scotia in thickets
and at the edges of woods.

Luzula multiflora
Common Woodrush

The Common Woodrush is abundant
throughout the province in fields,
barrens, and open woods. It is about
the same size as the Early Woodrush
but has more numerous and darker
flowers. Both of these species can be
distinguished from the numerous rushes
by the long hairs on their leaves and at
the nodes of their stems.

Sisyrinchium atlanticum
Eastern
Blue-eyed Grass

The bluish flowers of this and the next
species are familiar signs of spring. This
slender species is usually branched with
several flowers at the top of the stem. It is
limited to southwestern Nova Scotia, but is
common from Yarmouth to Lunenburg and
Annapolis counties where it grows in ditches and
around ponds and lakes.

Sisyrinchium montanum
Common Blue-eyed
Grass

The bluish flowers of this and the above
species are familiar signs of spring. This
species of Blue-eyed Grass grows to
between 20 and 30 cm tall and has stiff
narrow leaves and a single flower at the
top of its stem. The sepals and petals are
alike and both are coloured. It is very
common throughout the province in
fields, meadows, and open woods.

Trillium cernuum
Nodding Trillium

The Nodding Trillium blooms at the end of May and in early June. It is peculiar in that the flower is bent down under the whorl of leaves. The leaves themselves are wider than those of the other two species described here. The Nodding Trillium is common throughout central and northern Nova Scotia, rare on the Atlantic side, and absent in the four southwestern counties.

Trillium erectum
Purple Trillium

The whorl of three leaves and the reddish flowers with their three large petals easily identify this plant. **It is a rare plant and should not be picked.** The Purple Trillium is confined to the central part of the province, from Annapolis to Pictou County, but is most common along the southern slope of the North Mountain in the Annapolis Valley.

Trillium undulatum Painted Trillium

The Painted Trillium is the most common and earliest of our trilliums. The petals are white lined with pink stripes at their base. Painted Trillium can be identified by the three stalked leaves on its unbranched stem. These plants prefer open dryish woods. Although it is common on the mainland, it is rare in Cape Breton.

Uvularia sessilifolia Bellwort

These delicate plants are 30–40 cm tall, with yellow bell-like flowers that hang from the tip of the plant. It blooms towards the end of May. The Bellwort is found in rich woodlands or on alluvial soils, from Annapolis and Cumberland counties to Guysborough county; however, it has not been collected in Cape Breton in recent years.

Non-Woody (Herbaceous) Plants

DICOTS
Irregular flowers

Dicentra cucullaria
Dutchman's Breeches

This plant flowers during mid-May. It is very distinctive because of its finely divided leaves and the manner in which its two outer white petals are broadly spurred at the base to form the "legs" of the breeches. You can find Dutchman's Breeches in rich hardwoods and intervales from Kings County to northern Cape Breton.

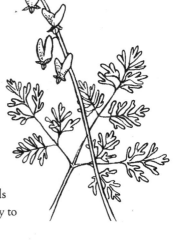

Glechoma hederacea
Ground-ivy, Gill

Ground-ivy is a weak trailing plant with small purplish flowers that first appear in early May. It is common throughout Nova Scotia in waste places and along roadsides, in gardens and lawns.

Veronica serpyllifolia
Thyme-leaved Speedwell

Thyme-leaved Speedwell is a low perennial, less than 10 cm tall, with small, slightly irregular flowers that are white with bluish lines. It is common throughout Nova Scotia, growing in lawns and flowering by the middle of May.

A Word about Violets

May is the month for violets. A number will begin flowering in May and some will continue during the summer.

Viola conspersa
Dog-violet

This is a leafy-stemmed violet, with the broad petals of the flower a light blue. The Dog-violet occurs frequently in damp fields and pastures from Digby and Cumberland counties to northern Cape Breton, and is often common in those areas. It is, however, absent in the southwestern part of the province and along the Atlantic coast.

Viola cucullata
Blue Violet

This is our most common and conspicuous blue violet. The colour varies from the usual violet to nearly white. A hand lens will allow positive identification by observing the clubbed hairs at the inner base of the lateral petals. It is found throughout Nova Scotia in meadows and around lakes and ponds through much of the summer.

Viola eriocarpa
Yellow Violet

This is our only yellow violet; it is easy to identify because of its tall leafy stem and wide leaves. The Yellow Violet is robust and is found from Annapolis County to northern Cape Breton. It occurs in rich hardwoods and along intervales, usually as scattered plants.

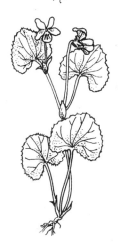

Viola incognita
Woodland Violet

The Woodland Violet flowers are white, much like the Small White Violet, but can be recognized by having one or both surfaces of its leaves more or less hairy. The Woodland Violet is very common in woods and thickets throughout Nova Scotia.

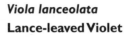

Viola lanceolata
Lance-leaved Violet

The flowers of the Lance-leaved Violet are white and appear during the early part of the season. The leaves are narrow in spring when the plants are in flower, but may be much wider later in the summer. This violet is common only in the southwestern part of the province; it becomes rarer in the Annapolis Valley and central Nova Scotia. It is found on low ground and near ponds and lakes.

Viola pallens
Small White Violet

The Small White Violet may be the first to flower and you can find its tiny white blossoms growing on moist ground at the edges of ponds and in meadows. The leaves are smooth on both sides. The Small White Violet is common throughout Nova Scotia.

Viola papilionacea
Cultivated Violet

This large, robust species is often grown as an ornamental and tends to escape. The flowers are large, whitish with purple veins.

Viola renifolia
Kidney-leaved Violet

This violet is also whitish with purple veins but can be recognized by the shape and texture of the leaves. These are typically kidney-shaped and are thick and firm in texture. The Kidney-leaved Violet prefers damp or cold woods, and is not uncommon along the sides of ravines and under conifers on gypsum. It is found from Digby to northern Cape Breton but is absent in southwestern Nova Scotia.

Viola septentrionalis
Northern Blue Violet

The Northern Blue Violet is the first blue violet observed in the spring. It tends to grow on light soils or in open woods. The plants are finely haired, and the lateral petals have the inside basal hairs straight instead of being clubbed as they are in *Viola cucullata*. Hybrids between these two species will be more difficult to identify. Early plants tend to have a slight reddish tinge. The Northern Blue Violet is common throughout the province.

Viola tricolor
Johnny-jump-up

The Johnny-jump-up flowers over a long season. This tiny pansy was originally introduced from Europe and is occasionally found as an escape to roadsides, fields and gardens. It is persistent and variously marked with yellow, purple, and white.

Non-Woody (Herbaceous) Plants

DICOTS
Regular flowers
White flowers

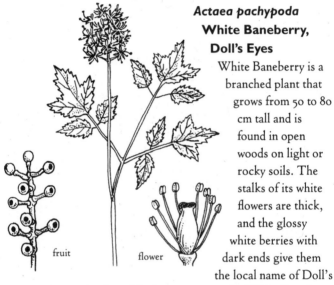

fruit

flower

Actaea pachypoda
**White Baneberry,
Doll's Eyes**

White Baneberry is a branched plant that grows from 50 to 80 cm tall and is found in open woods on light or rocky soils. The stalks of its white flowers are thick, and the glossy white berries with dark ends give them the local name of Doll's Eyes. The undersides of the leaves are smooth. White Baneberry is common from Annapolis County to northern Cape Breton, but rare in southwestern Nova Scotia and along the Atlantic coast.

fruit

flower cluster

flower

Actaea rubra
Red Baneberry

Red Baneberry appears similar to the White Baneberry. The white flowers, which appear in late May, are very small in a globular head. The berries of this plant are bright red and quite poisonous. Red Baneberry can be separated from White Baneberry, even in flower, because the leaves are finely hairy over the lower surface instead of being smooth. Red Baneberry has a distribution similar to White Baneberry.

Capsella bursa-pastoris
Shepherd's-purse

This winter annual may begin to flower in mid-spring. The tiny white flowers are produced at the top of the plant, while the purse-like fruits develop further back down the stem. Shepherd's-purse is common in gardens throughout the province.

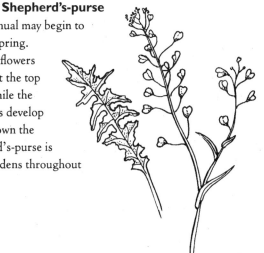

Cerastium vulgatum
Mouse-ear Chickweed

Mouse-ear Chickweed is a low sprawling plant with white flowers common throughout the province in fields, gardens, and lawns. The petals are only shallowly lobed and as long or shorter than the sepals. The plant is usually quite hairy.

Claytonia caroliniana
Spring-beauty

Spring-beauty is about 10 cm tall, often with its base buried in the leaf litter. The flowers are white or pinkish with deeper coloured lines. This delicate spring plant is found in deciduous woods from Annapolis and Cumberland counties eastward to Cape Breton; it is absent in southwestern Nova Scotia.

Coptis trifolia
Goldthread

Goldthread has small white flowers and its leaves have three evergreen lustrous leaflets. Brush the moss aside and the tangle of bright golden rootlets will suggest how it got its common name. Goldthread is found throughout Nova Scotia in bogs, with beds of them flowering in early May.

Dentaria diphylla
Toothwort

Toothwort is one of the few native plants of the Mustard Family and grows about 30–40 cm tall, with white flowers and the distinctive two opposite leaves. You can find Toothwort in rich moist soils in mixed or deciduous woods from Annapolis County and Cumberland County to Cape Breton, although it is absent in southwestern Nova Scotia.

Fragaria vesca
Woodland Strawberry

This slender plant produces white flowers and slender runners. The flowering stem is usually taller than the leaves. Characteristically, this strawberry has a beaded appearance because of the numerous seeds attached directly to the smooth surface. The Woodland Strawberry is usually found growing in shady areas and in ravines.

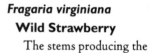

Fragaria virginiana
Wild Strawberry

The stems producing the white flowers of the Wild Strawberry are usually not taller than the leaves. Characteristically, this strawberry appears to have a pitted surface with the seeds embedded in the pits. Wild Strawberry is common throughout the province in fields, pastures, and open woodlands.

Houstonia caerulea
Bluets

Bluets tend to grow in patches, and they sometimes lend whole fields a pale lavender hue around the end of May or the first of June. The plant is usually unbranched; and the flower has only four petals. This tiny plant, less than 10 cm tall, is scattered in the western areas, is common around Halifax and Truro, and becomes rarer eastward.

Osmorhiza claytoni
Hairy Sweet Cicely

The umbels of Hairy Sweet Cicely are small with leafy bracts at the base and the flowers are small and white. The plant can then be identified by the softly hairy leaves and branched form. All the species of sweet cicely have elongated fruits. Hairy Sweet Cicely grows in deciduous woods and intervales from Annapolis County to Cape Breton, but it is rare on the Atlantic side.

Panax trifolius
Dwarf Ginseng

This slender plant grows from a small round tuber deep in the ground, flowering white at the end of May or in early June. The whorl of three leaves, each with three leaflets, makes it distinctive. It grows in wet woods or on intervales, scattered in north-central Nova Scotia.

Petasites palmatus
Sweet Coltsfoot

Sweet Coltsfoot's flowers appear in late May or early June and are whitish with very short rays. The leaves appear later from the base of the flowering stem. Sweet Coltsfoot is scattered in swampy woods and recent clearings and is most common in the north-central part of the province.

Potentilla tridentata
Three-toothed Cinquefoil

The thick wedge-shaped leaflets with the three teeth will serve to identify the Three-toothed Cinquefoil. It has white flowers from late May or early June onward. It is a low plant, usually less than 10 cm tall, growing in exposed locations such as headlands, cliffs, and rocky outcrops. It is common around the whole coast but rarer inland.

Sagina procumbens
Pearlwort

The flower parts of this small plant usually occur in whorls of four. The tiny white petals are not lobed and are shorter than the sepals.
Pearlwort is found throughout the province, growing in damp areas of lawns, fields, and pastures.

Stellaria graminea
Stitchwort

Stitchwort is a chickweed and one of the common plants that begin to grow one year and flower and produce seed the following. This chickweed is one of the first to flower. The flowers are white. Note how the 5 petals are divided almost to the base, so that the number appears to be 10.

Stellaria media
Common Chickweed

The small white flowers have petals that are divided almost to the base. The leaves appear almost egg-shaped in outline and are, therefore, wider than those of the Stitchwort. Common Chickweed is found throughout the province.

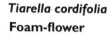

Tiarella cordifolia
Foam-flower

This slender perennial, about 20 cm tall, has a foamy raceme of white flowers. The anthers of the stamens may be either yellow or bright orange. Foam-flower is found in the richest deciduous woods from Kings County to Pictou County; it is scattered around Truro near the intervales.

Trientalis borealis
Star-flower

Star-flower is one of our better-known woodland plants. The plants are usually found alone and grow about 20 cm tall. The single whorl of leaves on the stem and the white star-like flowers make it easy to identify. It is found in mixed woods throughout Nova Scotia and flowers in late May or early June.

Non-Woody (Herbaceous) Plants

DICOTS
Regular Flowers
Yellow flowers

Barbarea vulgaris
Yellow Rocket

Yellow Rocket usually occurs as individual
plants but occasionally an entire field may
be yellow with it in late May or early June.
Yellow Rocket is much like Wild Radish,
but the whole plant is smooth and the
surface is shiny. It is
common along rivers
and in waste places and
fields.

lower
leaves

Caltha palustris
Marsh-marigold

Marsh-marigold is a
rare plant. Its clear
yellow flowers look like
large showy buttercups,
but its leaves are much larger
and thicker. It is usually found at
the edge of shallow ponds, where it
flowers in late May or early June. It
is most frequently found along the
Northumberland coast and up to northern Inverness County.

59

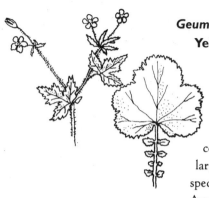

Geum macrophyllum
Yellow Avens

This yellow-flowered species is one of the first geums to bloom in the spring. The terminal leaflet of its compound leaf is much larger than those of other species of geum. Yellow Avens grows from Annapolis County to Cape Breton but is rare on the Atlantic side of the province. It grows in rich or alluvial soils.

Hieracium pilosella
Mouse-ear Hawkweed

Mouse-ear Hawkweed is a low plant, about 10 cm high, and is the first of many hawkweeds to bloom in the spring; it is common on light soils and becomes conspicuous in late May and early June. It has abundant runners and its yellow flowering heads are borne singly. Sometimes Mouse-ear Hawkweed hybridizes with another low species and the resulting plants are larger and greener, often with several flowers on a stalk. Abundant throughout the province, Mouse-ear Hawkweed is especially prevalent in eastern Nova Scotia.

Oxalis stricta
Yellow
Wood-sorrel

Yellow Wood-sorrel is a small
erect annual with three leaflets
like a shamrock. Its yellow
flowers are erect and bell-like,
and its fruits are elongate and
point straight upward. It is
common throughout the province
around towns and gardens and
begins to flower at the end of May.

Potentilla anserina
Silverweed

Silverweed's showy yellow
flowers grow one to a stalk
and the plant can be
recognized by its
numerous leaflets.
The young stolons
run freely over
the soil so that the
plant tends to
grow in patches.

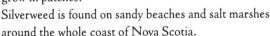

Silverweed is found on sandy beaches and salt marshes
around the whole coast of Nova Scotia.

Potentilla argentea
Silvery Cinquefoil

The Silvery Cinquefoil is scattered in waste places and dry fields. The flowers are yellow and the leaves are so densely hairy that they appear silvery beneath. It is abundant throughout the province.

Potentilla norvegica
Rough Cinquefoil

Rough Cinquefoil plants are roughly hairy and have small yellow flowers. It is common throughout Nova Scotia, usually present but rarely abundant.

Potentilla recta
Cinquefoil

This plant grows to about a metre tall, with yellow flowers, and may be identified by the five to seven leaflets attached at one point on the leaf stalk. It is becoming more common, and scattered plants appear along roadsides and in fields.

Potentilla simplex
Cinquefoil

This Cinquefoil is the
earliest to bloom and
the smallest of our
Potentillas. When it
begins to flower at the
end of May, it resembles a
small yellow strawberry.
On poor or leached soil, it
may form a mat over the
ground. Scattered throughout
the province, it is more commonly found
in central Nova Scotia.

Ranunculus
abortivus
Wood
Buttercup

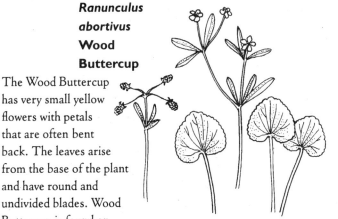

The Wood Buttercup
has very small yellow
flowers with petals
that are often bent
back. The leaves arise
from the base of the plant
and have round and
undivided blades. Wood
Buttercup is found on
wooded hillsides and intervales from Digby and Cumberland
counties to northern Cape Breton. Sometimes the Wood
Buttercup appears in early spring; such plants may be dwarfed
and have miniature flowers.

Raphanus raphanistrum
Wild Radish, Charlock

Wild Radish begins to flower in late May. It can be distinguished from Wild Mustard and related species by its paler yellow flowers, jointed seed pods, and more hairy leaves. Wild Radish also has erect sepals, while Wild Mustard, for example, has sepals that spread horizontally. Wild Radish is especially common in the Annapolis Valley, but is also common elsewhere.

fruit

Sinapsis arvensis
Wild Mustard

The Wild Mustard has only recently been introduced and is still rather rare, but the bright yellow flowers are conspicuous when present. This plant is much like the Wild Radish, but the seed pods split longitudinally when ripe; the sepals spread horizontally rather than standing erect. Wild Mustard is found in scattered patches throughout the province.

fruit

Taraxacum officinale
Dandelion

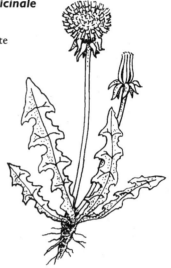

Dandelions begin to flower in late May. The yellow flowers have many rays and occur singly on hollow unbranched stalks. The leaves are variously lobed but are not hairy like those of the Fall Dandelion. Dandelion is common throughout Nova Scotia in lawns, pastures, and cultivated soil.

Non-Woody (Herbaceous) Plants

DICOTS
Regular flowers
Greenish-yellow flowers

Caulophyllum thalictroides
Blue Cohosh

Blue Cohosh, with yellow-green or purplish flowers, is a perennial plant about a metre high, scattered in deciduous woods. The best way to identify it is by the distinctive shape of the leaflets. The plant is very rare in Nova Scotia, although it is known from central Kings County, around Truro, and in central Cape Breton.

Non-Woody (Herbaceous) Plants

DICOTS
Regular flowers
Blue flowers

Aquilegia
vulgaris
Garden
Columbine

The flowers are nodding, with the five petals extending backwards from their base to form long spurs. The flowers are large and few in number. Double flowers and various colours are occasionally seen. Columbine is a garden escape found in many parts of the province; it may persist in rich soil in damp hollows and shady locations.

Myosotis scorpioides
Forget-me-not

Forget-me-nots are sprawling plants with tiny blue flowers. The flowers first appear in a coiled inflorescence, which becomes straight as the flowers open. Common in ditches, meadows and along brooks, they often grow in large masses.

Non-Woody (Herbaceous) Plants

DICOTS
Regular flowers
Pinkish or red flowers

Geum rivale
Purple Avens

Purple Avens' purplish or purple-veined nodding flowers are conspicuous in meadows and at the edge of swamps. It is most showy as it comes into flower. Its bell-like flowers, divided leaves, and height of between 30 and 50 cm serve to identify it. Purple Avens is found throughout the province.

Lychnis flos-cuculi
Ragged Robin

Its distinctive deep pink colour (white varieties are known) and finely lobed petals make Ragged Robin easy to identify. It is abundant in the centre of the Annapolis Valley, where entire meadows may be red when it is in flower in late May or early June. Only scattered patches occur elsewhere, where it may be locally established in meadows.

lobed petals

Phlox subulata
Ground Pink, Moss Pink

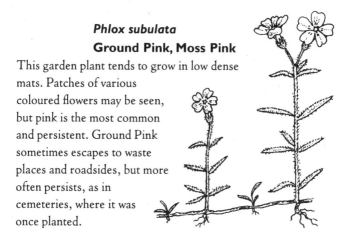

This garden plant tends to grow in low dense mats. Patches of various coloured flowers may be seen, but pink is the most common and persistent. Ground Pink sometimes escapes to waste places and roadsides, but more often persists, as in cemeteries, where it was once planted.

Rumex acetosella
Sheep-sorrel

Sheep-sorrel plants are low and slender with very tiny flowers, which tend to be pale reddish. It is common all over Nova Scotia and is best identified by the outline of its leaves. A slightly sour taste is typical.

Woody Plants

TREES

Acer pseudo-platanus
Sycamore Maple

The Sycamore Maple has large and drooping yellowish-green flower clusters appearing by mid-June. It is only occasionally planted or seen as an escape, in Nova Scotia.

Acer spicatum
Mountain Maple

The Mountain Maple is a common small tree with reddish-purple young twigs and the underside of the leaves lightly hairy. It is most conspicuous in June, when in flower, because its erect clusters of tiny, pale greenish flowers are often very numerous. It is common throughout the province, especially along the Bay of Fundy and in northern Cape Breton.

Fraxinus americana
White Ash

The greenish flowers of the White Ash appear with or before the leaves. The male trees produce only staminate flowers with the stamens in clusters; the female trees produce only carpellate flowers in a looser group. There are no petals and the sepals are minute. A distinguishing feature of the White Ash is the opposite buds and leaves; its compound leaves have from five to nine leaflets.

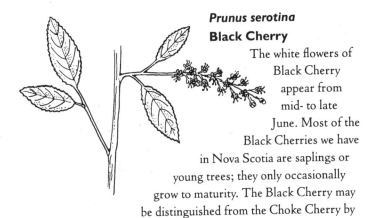

Prunus serotina
Black Cherry

The white flowers of Black Cherry appear from mid- to late June. Most of the Black Cherries we have in Nova Scotia are saplings or young trees; they only occasionally grow to maturity. The Black Cherry may be distinguished from the Choke Cherry by the firm in-turned teeth on the margins of its leaves.

Prunus virginiana
Choke Cherry

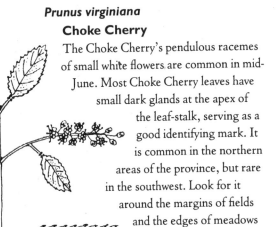

The Choke Cherry's pendulous racemes of small white flowers are common in mid-June. Most Choke Cherry leaves have small dark glands at the apex of the leaf-stalk, serving as a good identifying mark. It is common in the northern areas of the province, but rare in the southwest. Look for it around the margins of fields and the edges of meadows and along stone walls.

Woody Plants

SHRUBS

Stems with spines or prickles

Rosa carolina
Pasture Rose

The blossoms of this rose occur in various shades of red. This is probably the earliest flowering rose in the province. As the common name implies, it is usually found growing on well-drained pasture lands.

Rosa cinnamomea
Cinnamon Rose

The flowers of Cinnamon Rose are double, making this early rose easy to distinguish from other wild roses. They are very prickly with curved spines. Other common roses flower by the end of June. Cinnamon Rose is usually found around old homesteads and along roadsides. It is believed to be a hybrid rose by some authorities.

Rosa multiflora
Multi-flowered
Rose

This rose is fairly easy
to identify because of
its numerous small
white blossoms. The
plant has been used for
hedges and may still be
found associated with older
dwelling sites.

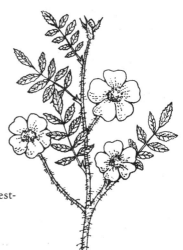

Rosa nitida
Swamp
Rose

This reddish rose commonly
grows in association with
swampy thickets, spruce
swamps, peat mats, and
bogs. Although it occurs
throughout the province,
Swamp Rose appears to be
especially abundant in southwestern Nova Scotia.

Rosa virginiana
Common Wild Rose
The blossoms of this rose occur
in variable shades of red. The
plants are robust and stout, and
may be found in a variety of
habitats throughout the province.

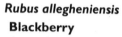

Rubus allegheniensis
Blackberry
All the members of
this group have white
flowers and leaves
with a number of
leaflets attached at
one point. Otherwise
they are quite variable.
This is a stout erect blackberry producing edible fruits.
The canes are very prickly, and
the inflorescence is covered with
numerous glandular hairs.

Rubus canadensis **Bramble**

A tall erect or arching blackberry with scattered prickles or spines on the canes. Its stems may be smooth or slightly prickled and it is nearly as abundant as the *Rubus allegheniensis*. The flowers are white; the fruit is small.

Rubus hispidus **Trailing Blackberry**

This group is very variable with white flowers. All our trailing blackberries are included here. The smallest type, after which the group is named, is a slender form found in bogs. It has three leaflets to each leaf and is ever-green.

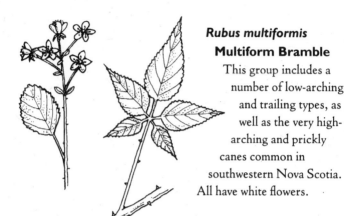

Rubus multiformis
Multiform Bramble
This group includes a number of low-arching and trailing types, as well as the very high-arching and prickly canes common in southwestern Nova Scotia. All have white flowers.

Rubus strigosus
Raspberry
Some of these raspberries are more prickly than others. The arrangement of the leaflets on the leaf is quite different from that in the blackberries. The flowers are white or greenish-white. This is similar to the Cultivated Raspberry and is often very common after a fire or when land is being cleared.

Woody Plants

SHRUBS

Stems without spines or prickles
Flowers bell-shaped

Gaylussacia baccata
Huckleberry

The reddish flowers are inconspicuous and appear in early June. The shrub is much like a large blueberry, but can be distinguished from them because the undersides of Huckleberry leaves are dotted with yellowish glands. The leaves are relatively thin, tapered at both ends. The berries are small and black but of good flavour. You can find Huckleberry scattered throughout Nova Scotia, but it is abundant in the southwestern part of the province where it may grow to 2 m high.

Gaylussacia dumosa
Bog Huckleberry

The inconspicuous reddish flowers appear in early June. The leaves are thick and oval-shaped with glandular structures appearing as yellow dots on the underside. The fruits are similar to blueberries but are hairy. The Bog Huckleberry may be found throughout the province in association with boggy barrens and peat bogs.

79

Vaccinium angustifolium
Lowbush Blueberry

This is the common blueberry of our fields and barrens. The blueberries begin to flower in early June; the flowers are white or white tinged with pink. Upon close examination, note that the leaves are hairy along the midrib.

Vaccinium corymbosum
Highbush Blueberry

The Highbush Blueberry is mainly identified by its greater size and larger leaves. Its white or pinkish flowers are also more showy than those of our other blueberries. Tall bushes may be several metres tall, but it can also cross with other species, and half-high bushes are frequently found. Look for the Highbush Blueberry on rocky barrens, in wet pastures, and along lakeshores. It is common in southwestern Nova Scotia but unknown in other parts of the province.

Vaccinium myrtilloides
Velvet-leaf Blueberry

The leaves of this blueberry are softly hairy, and the plant is most often found in shaded locations. The fruits are usually more scattered and smaller than those of the Lowbush Blueberry. The Velvet-leaf Blueberry is common throughout Nova Scotia in dry soils, thickets, and open woods.

Vaccinium vitis-idaea
Foxberry

The upright branches are
less than 10 cm tall with a few
flowers at the tip. The pink
flowers appear during early June;
its berries are red. The Foxberry is
common in the cooler regions of the
province, seldom fruiting inland.

Andromeda glaucophylla
Andromeda

The small white waxy flowers of
Andromeda are perfectly bell-shaped.
The leaves are narrow with the edge in-
turned and with a very sharp point at
the tip. Andromeda is scattered in peat
bogs throughout the province, usually
half buried in the peat moss.

Woody Plants

SHRUBS

Stems without spines or prickles
Flowers not bell-shaped
White flowers

Cornus alternifolia
Alternate-leaved Dogwood

The white-flowered Alternate-leaved Dogwood is much taller than Red Osier Dogwood and may even grow into a small tree. The flower parts are in fours and the veins of the leaf curve towards the tip. The buds and leaves alternate. This species tends to be a woodland plant, found in rich woodlands from northern Digby County to northern Cape Breton.

Cornus stolonifera
Red Osier Dogwood

Red Osier Dogwood is a branching shrub 1–2 m tall that has reddish bark in the early spring. The flowers are white. Note that the buds and leaves are opposite on the stem, while other species of *Cornus* have them alternate. The flower-parts are in fours, and the veins of the leaf curve around towards the tip. Most common in rich and alkaline soils, Red Osier Dogwood is generally absent from the southwestern regions of the province.

Ledum groenlandicum
Labrador Tea

Labrador Tea flowers in June with masses of white bloom. The undersides of the leaves of this shrub are rusty-woolly, with the margins inrolled. It is a bush from 50 to 80 cm tall and grows in wet pastures and bogs, scattered throughout Nova Scotia.

Rubus chamaemorus
Bake-apple, Cloudberry

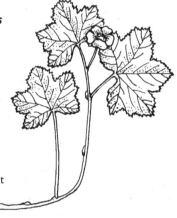

The Bake-apple has white flowers like those of a blackberry, but is less than 10 cm tall. It is found in peat bogs and is common on headlands around the coast of much of mainland Nova Scotia, except it is relatively rare in the southwestern part of the province. Although the plants appear to be herbaceous, the base is actually woody.

Rubus pubescens
Dewberry

Dewberry is a long smooth trailing plant that usually forms patches that cover the ground. It has three leaflets. The white flowers are small; the berries are bright red, watery, and very tasty. It grows from Yarmouth to Cape Breton, although it is rare along the Atlantic side of the province. Look for Dewberry on low or boggy land, along talus slopes, and on intervales.

Woody Plants

SHRUBS

Stems without spines or prickles
Flowers not bell-shaped
Yellow flowers

Hudsonia ericoides
Hudsonia

This small bushy plant is only about 20
cm tall, with needle-like leaves and
bright yellow flowers during June.
Hudsonia flowers are abundant,
and each one has numerous stamens.
It is conspicuous on the sands of the
Annapolis Valley and on rocky soils
and sandy barrens in Shelburne and
western Halifax counties.

Rhamnus cathartica
Common Buckthorn

The Buckthorn's flowers are small and yellowish, with four petals
and four stamens. The plant has branches that become thorn-like
and the thick leaves have veins that curve
prominently towards the tip of the leaf.

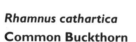

The berries are black and mildly
poisonous. Buckthorn used
to be planted as a hedge
plant and has
escaped in some
areas of the
province.

Woody Plants

SHRUBS

Stems without spines or prickles
Flowers not bell-shaped
Green flowers

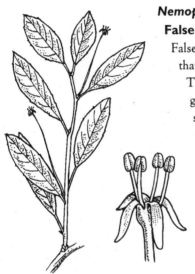

Nemopanthus mucronata
False Holly

False Holly grows as a shrub
that is often 5 m or so tall.
The False Holly's small
greenish flowers are on long
slender stalks. Its leaves are
thin and pale on the lower
side with a tiny sharp point
at the tip. It is common
throughout Nova Scotia
and is rarely absent in wet
woods or at the edges of
bogs and in barrens.

Woody Plants

SHRUBS

Stems without spines or prickles
Flowers not bell-shaped
Pinkish or purple flowers

Kalmia angustifolia
Lambkill

Lambkill is a very common shrub, less than 50 cm tall, with clusters of pinkish saucer-like flowers, located partially down the stem away from the tip, that appear about the middle of June. The leaves are smooth, tough, and evergreen. Lambkill grows in patches in pastures, barrens and along roadsides throughout Nova Scotia. It often grows in blueberry fields.

Kalmia polifolia
Pale Laurel

The Pale Laurel, often found as individual plants, is similar in appearance to Lambkill and conspicuous only when it is in flower. Pale Laurel is a small neat plant with saucer-shaped pinkish flowers in clusters at the tips, and with the leaves slightly inrolled and whitish hairy beneath. Pale Laurel is scattered in peat bogs throughout the province.

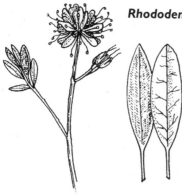

Rhododendron canadense
Rhodora

Rhodora is one of the most prominent of our early-flowering shrubs, and whole areas may be rose-purple as it comes into bloom at the end of May or in early June. The flower is very irregular, with the top three petals joined together, and the two lower ones flaring to the side. Rhodora is common throughout the province in swamps, bogs, and wet pastures.

Syringa vulgaris
Lilac

For years Lilac has been widely planted as an ornamental shrub; the form with lilac-purple flowers is the common one. The flowers have four petals and four stamens. Lilac can persist indefinitely around old houses and along roadsides, where clumps of it may occasionally be seen.

Vaccinium oxycoccos
Small Cranberry

The pinkish flowers of the Small Cranberry appear towards the end of June. The flowering stalks have a pair of bracts less than 1 mm wide; the leaves are less than a centimetre long, often with their margins inrolled. Its ripe berries are small, ovoid, reddish-purple, and sometimes dotted with brown. Less common than the larger cranberry, the Small Cranberry is found throughout the province in bogs and swamps, almost always associated with peat moss.

Non-Woody (Herbaceous) Plants

MONOCOTS

Flowers in a fleshy spike, partly surrounded by a leafy bract

Arisaema stewardsonii
Jack-in-the-pulpit

The Jack-in-the-pulpit's three leaflets to a leaf, green/purple flowers, and its distinctive flowering structure are like that of no other plant. It is found in wet woods and on alluvial soils and is common from Yarmouth County along the northern side of the province to the Margaree Valley in Cape Breton.

Calla palustris
Water Arum, Wild Calla

The Wild Calla is conspicuous when it is in flower, since the large bract behind the spike of its yellowish-white flowers is a glossy white. Its leaves are thick and smooth, and its thick stem commonly grows out of the water. It is often found in bogs and at the margins of swamps. It occurs only rarely in southwestern Nova Scotia but is scattered throughout the rest of the province to north-central Cape Breton.

Non-Woody (Herbaceous) Plants

MONOCOTS
Irregular flowers
Various colours: white, pink, yellow, purplish-green

Arethusa bulbosa
Arethusa

This most orchid-like of our smaller flowers grows on a leafless stem 20–30 cm tall from a round bulb hidden in the peat moss. The flower is pinkish, spotted, and streaked with purple and flowers beginning in early June. The one basal leaf arises later. The Arethusa is found in peat bogs, around the whole coast of Nova Scotia.

Corallorhiza trifida
Early Coral-root

Early Coral-root has a pale yellow-green colour because it completely lacks chlorophyll. The plant is slender, 10–30 cm tall, and has a number of small orchid-like flowers with white, unspotted lips. It is scattered from Annapolis and Cumberland counties to northern Cape Breton in coniferous woods.

Cypripedium acaule
Common Lady's-slipper

The large slipper-like flowers of the Common Lady's-slipper occur singly at the top of stout stems, which grow about 30 cm tall. There are two nearly opposite leaves. You can find Common Lady's-slippers with white flowers, but pink flowers occur more frequently. This plant is scattered throughout the province.

Cypripedium calceolus
Yellow Lady's-slipper

The Yellow Lady's-slipper has smaller flowers than the Common Lady's-slipper, and several yellow flowers may be produced on a single plant. Its flowers appear in early June. The Yellow Lady's-slipper is becoming one of our rare plants. It is found sparingly from King's County east to Cape Breton in deciduous woods, most commonly near outcrops of gypsum.

Listera cordata
Heart-leaved Twayblade

The Heart-leaved Twayblade is quite a rare plant.
It is very slender, grows from 10 to 20 cm tall, and
has insignificant purplish-green flowers and a pair
of opposite leaves midway along the stem. Occasionally, Heart-leaved Twayblade occurs in damp or
coniferous woods throughout the province but
is often overlooked. It is more common near
the coast and in northern Cape Breton.

Pogonia ophioglossoides
Rose Pogonia

This delicate orchid grows about 30
cm tall, with a single pinkish flower at
the top and one or two smooth leaves
on the stem. Its lower petal is fringed.
You can find the Rose Pogonia from late
June onward in peat bogs and meadows and
along lake-shores. It often grows in profusion
near the Atlantic coast but is rare elsewhere.

Non-Woody (Herbaceous) Plants

MONOCOTS
Regular flowers
White flowers

Allium tricoccum
Wild Leek

The Wild Leek is peculiar in that its leaves appear in early spring and disappear before the flowers are produced in June. The leaves are wide and a smooth green throughout, growing from egg-shaped bulbs. The flowers are greenish-white and grow in umbels. The whole plant has a strong onion-like odour and taste. It is common in Kings and Colchester counties, and in Cape Breton, but may be scattered throughout in deciduous forests.

Maianthemum canadense Wild Lily-of-the-valley

Wild Lily-of-the-valley is common in coniferous woods. The white flowers in a small raceme bloom in late May and early June. It usually has two leaves that are heart-shaped at the base and the petals and stamens occur in fours. This plant is common throughout the province.

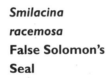

Smilacina racemosa False Solomon's Seal

This unbranched plant with a slightly zig-zag stem grows about 50 cm tall with a branched raceme of tiny white flowers. False Solomon's Seal appears in early June in open deciduous woods. It is rare in southwestern Nova Scotia but becoming more common northward.

Smilacina stellata
Starry False Solomon's Seal

Starry False Solomon's Seal is stiffly
erect with numerous leaves. The
small white flowers, as in all the
Solomon's Seals, have six showy parts
to the flower and also six stamens. Its
distribution is rather local, on
headlands or on slopes leading down
to the sea. It flowers in mid-June.

Smilacina trifolia
Three-leaved False Solomon's Seal

The Three-leaved False
Solomon's Seal, with white
flowers, is smaller but
otherwise resembles the
preceding two species. It
usually grows with the base of
the plant buried in peat moss.
Three-leaved False Solomon's
Seal is common throughout Nova
Scotia in bogs, swamps, and wet
meadows.

Non-Woody (Herbaceous) Plants

MONOCOTS
Regular flowers
Yellow or greenish flowers

Asparagus officinalis
Garden Asparagus

Garden Asparagus appears as a single-stemmed plant, a metre or more tall, and occurs only in gardens or as an escape. Its leaves are reduced to bracts, and each bract has a group of tiny leaf-like stems in its axil. Its small greenish-white flowers are produced singly or in pairs on slender stalks at the base of the main branches.

Clintonia borealis
Bluebead Lily

The Bluebead Lily is about 30 cm tall and flowers in early June. Its several yellow flowers are borne at the tip of the stem, while all its smooth wide leaves are found at the base of the plant. These leaves resemble the leaves of Wild Leek but without the distinct onion taste. Bluebead Lily is very common throughout the province in deciduous or mixed woods and often grows in patches. The poisonous fruits turn a dark blue.

97

Medeola virginiana
Indian Cucumber-root

This slender plant grows about 40 cm tall with two distinct whorls of leaves. Its small yellow flowers are curved down under the upper whorl. Indian Cucumber-root blooms from mid-June onward. It can be found scattered from Yarmouth County to Guysborough County but is common in open woods from Annapolis and Cumberland counties to northern Cape Breton.

Polygonatum pubescens
Hairy Solomon's Seal

Hairy Solomon's Seal is a rather coarse plant, with its inconspicuous greenish flowers often produced in pairs. The minute hairs associated with the veins on the underside of the leaves are a distinguishing feature of Hairy Solomon's Seal. The plant is found only in the richest deciduous woods, along the margins of intervales, or in ravines. It is found in such habitats from Annapolis County to northern Cape Breton but is rare elsewhere.

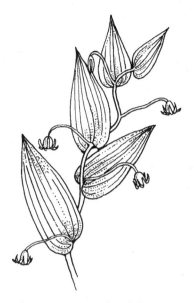

Streptopus amplexifolius
Green Twisted-stalk

Green Twisted-stalk is not as common as its earlier blooming
cousin Rose Mandarin (*Streptopus roseus*, see p. 101). It has
greenish-white flowers with widely spreading lobes. The leaves
clasp the stem at their base, and their blades have smooth
margins. Green Twisted-stalk is rare in the southwestern
counties but common from Annapolis County to northern Cape
Breton.

Non-Woody (Herbaceous) Plants

MONOCOTS
Regular flowers
Blue flowers

Iris setosa
Beach Blue Flag

The erect petals of this blue flower are tubular. The narrow leaves are usually between 5 and 10 mm wide. This plant is found near beaches throughout the province.

Iris versicolor
Blue Flag

Blue Flag, a species of Iris, is a familiar flower in late spring/early summer. The erect petals of this blue flower are flat, and the stiff leaves are usually between 5 and 30 mm wide. This plant grows abundantly throughout the province along streams and in swamps and meadows.

Non-Woody (Herbaceous) Plants

MONOCOTS
Regular flowers
Pinkish or red flowers

Allium schoenoprasum
Chives

Chives' flowers are rose-coloured, and its leaves are linear. It shares the onion-like characteristics of its cousin the Wild Leek. Chives is a rare plant and is found mainly along the Bay of Fundy and in northern Inverness County on low land and headlands near the coast.

Streptopus roseus
Twisted-stalk,
Rose Mandarin

This plant is scattered to common throughout Nova Scotia in mixed and open coniferous woods. It grows with two main branches and pink flowers. The margins of the leaf blade are finely ciliate.

Non-Woody (Herbaceous) Plants

DICOTS
Irregular flowers
Various colours
Blue, white, red, yellow, purple

Ajuga reptans
Bugle

Bugle is a low garden escape, 20–30 cm tall, with loose erect spikes of blue flowers. It is found in lawns and gardens and, since it has numerous runners, it tends to grow in patches and spread over considerable areas. The flowers are tubular with the lower petals, much larger than the others, forming a lip. Bugle is a low creeping garden escape, scattered in and around established communities.

Lathyrus japonicus
Beach Pea

Beach Pea usually grows in mats and forms abundant pods from its pea-like flowers. This pea plant, with the wide leaflets and the bluish flowers, is common around our coast on sandy or gravelly beaches and is perhaps our most common coastal plant.

Lupinus nootkatensis
Nootkaten Lupin

This lupin has only 6 to 10 leaflets to a leaf, and these are densely hairy on the undersides; otherwise it is much like the following species. *Lupinus nootkatensis* is abundant along the Lupin Trail at Chebogue Point, Yarmouth County.

Lupinus polyphyllus
Garden Lupin

The Garden Lupin is a showy ornamental that frequently escapes to roadsides and meadows. Its tall spike-like group of flowers and its leaves with many leaflets attached at one point are distinctive. The

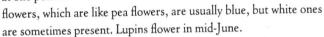

flowers, which are like pea flowers, are usually blue, but white ones are sometimes present. Lupins flower in mid-June.

Medicago lupulina
Black Medick

Black Medick is usually low and sprawling. Its small size, together with its stalked terminal leaflets, make Black Medick distinctive. Its tiny yellow pea-like flowers are arranged in a short head that is quite different from those of the yellow clovers, which appear later. The flowers form slightly curved or twisted fruits. Black Medick is an annual and common throughout the province in waste places, in gardens and along roadsides.

Prunella vulgaris
Heal-all, Self-heal

Heal-all is a low plant of grassy habitats, 10–30 cm tall, with small and irregular blue flowers arranged in a short thick spike, and oval overlapping bracts. No other plant has such a short, condensed spike. Pinkish flowers may occasionally be seen. Heal-all is common throughout the Province.

Rhinanthus crista-galli
Yellow Rattle

Yellow Rattle's very irregular flowers appear about the middle of June, and its inflated capsules are typical later. Yellow Rattle is common in run-out fields, but it is only scattered in other habitats. It seldom grows taller than 10 cm, and its unbranched stems have black lines along them.

Trifolium hybridum
Alsike Clover

Alsike Clover is exten-
sively grown as a forage crop and also used for roadside planting. Alsike Clover is smaller than Red Clover, its leaves are smooth, and its flowers are white with only a tinge of red. It is common throughout the province.

Trifolium pratense
Red Clover

The clovers begin to flower about the middle of June and are soon abundant in fields and meadows. Red Clover leaves are hairy, and its leaflets are longer than those of the other species. It is scattered to common throughout the province.

Trifolium repens
Creeping White Clover

Creeping White Clover flowers are white and its leaflets often have a notch at the tip, while the leaflets of Alsike Clover are more pointed. The Creeping White Clover's low creeping habit will sometimes help you to identify it, although this is often a difficult feature to see. It is abundant throughout the province and often occurs in lawns. Note that all the clovers have three leaflets to a leaf.

Veronica arvensis
Field Speedwell

There are many kinds of Speedwells, but most flower later in the summer. All have slightly irregular flowers in which the two upper petals are joined to make one petal slightly larger than the side or lower petals. Field Speedwell is a rough, hairy plant about 10 cm tall with small bluish flowers. The fruits are typically heart-shaped and divided into two halves. It grows in dry fields and waste places, often on sandy soils throughout the province.

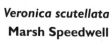

Veronica scutellata
Marsh Speedwell

Marsh Speedwell has long narrow leaves, and its flowers are pale violet. It flowers from mid-June onward. As with Field Speedwell, the fruits are heart-shaped and divided down the middle. This low species grows in shallow water, in ditches, or in shallow ponds and is common in the northern and central parts of the province.

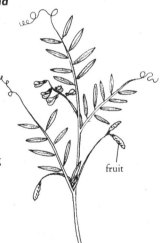

Vicia cracca
Tufted Vetch

Tufted Vetch is identified by its
small, blue, pea-like flowers and its
numerous leaflets to a leaf, with the
terminal ones modified to form
tendrils. It flowers from early June
onward. Several species of vetch bloom
later during the year. Tufted Vetch is our
most common vetch and is scattered to
abundant throughout the province in old fields and about towns.

Vicia tetrasperma
Slender Vetch

This very slender vetch, which
is the smallest of our vetches,
grows only about 10 cm tall
and has very tiny, pale blue
flowers. It is an annual whose
pods contain only four seeds
each. It occurs frequently in the
Annapolis Valley and is becoming
more common elsewhere.

fruit

Non-Woody (Herbaceous) Plants

DICOTS
Regular flowers
White flowers

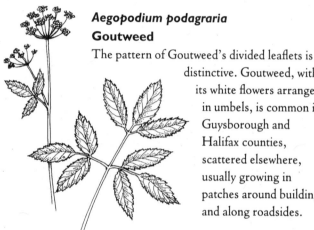

Aegopodium podagraria
Goutweed

The pattern of Goutweed's divided leaflets is distinctive. Goutweed, with its white flowers arranged in umbels, is common in Guysborough and Halifax counties, scattered elsewhere, usually growing in patches around buildings and along roadsides.

Anemone quinquefolia
Anemone

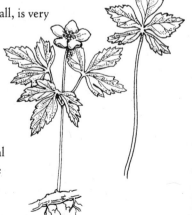

This delicate plant, 10–30 cm tall, is very rare. Two to five leaves occur in a whorl near the top of the Anemone's stem and usually only one flower is present. This flower has no petals but its five sepals are showy and usually white. It is found in intervale woods in north-central Nova Scotia and flowers in late May and early June.

Antennaria neodioica
Everlasting,
Smaller Pussy-toes

Everlasting is common in June when both
hairy-leaved and smooth forms may be
found. The flowering heads of Everlasting
are ragged, and the individual white
flowers are inconspicuous. The genus
grows about 10 cm tall but is variable,
and patches of Everlasting may be
quite different in appearance from
one location to another. Everlasting
grows in patches on the sterile soil of
worn pastures, barrens, and roadside
banks throughout the province.

Anthriscus sylvestris
Wild Chervil

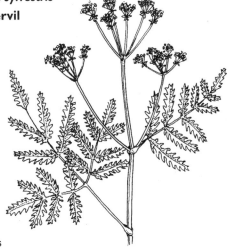

This introduced
plant usually
grows in masses
up to a metre tall
and flowers in
mid-June. Its
large compound
leaves and the oval
bracts at the base
of its small umbels
of white flowers
help to identify
this plant. The fruits
are elongated. Wild Chervil
is spreading rapidly in Colchester County and Cape Breton.

Aralia nudicaulis
Wild Sarsaparilla

Wild Sarsaparilla has umbels of tiny white perfect flowers arranged in threes. It grows 30–40 cm tall in dry woods and old forests. Its leaves have three main horizontal divisions and its flowering stems are separate, arising directly from the ground. Wild Sarsaparilla grows throughout the province and is one of our most common woodland plants of late spring and early summer.

Arenaria lateriflora
Sandwort

Sandwort is a wiry upright chickweed with unlobed petals. It is only about 10 cm tall with white flowers. The stems and leaves may be covered with numerous minute hairs. You can find it scattered throughout Nova Scotia in meadows and thickets and on exposed headlands.

Cardamine pratensis
Cuckoo-flower

Cuckoo-flower was originally introduced in grass seed and meadows may now be white with it in early June. Leaves produced near the tip have leaflets that appear linear; leaves produced lower on the stem have leaflets that are larger and more rounded. Cuckoo-flower is a member of the Mustard Family and its flower parts are arranged in fours. It is common in meadows in the Annapolis Valley and is slowly spreading elsewhere.

Carum carvi
Caraway

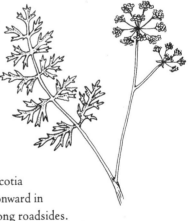

The Caraway plant may have many branches, grows up to 50 cm tall, and has several umbels of small white flowers, often with a slightly pinkish tinge. It is much like the later-flowering Wild Carrot, but it is smooth instead of hairy. Caraway is common throughout Nova Scotia and flowers from early June onward in damp fields, meadows and along roadsides.

Cerastium arvense
Field Chickweed

Field Chickweed is a conspicuous plant with white flowers, in which the petals are much longer than the sepals. Its petals show the same shallow lobing at their tips that is characteristic of so many plants of this family. The stems may be covered with minute hairs. Originally, Field Chickweed was introduced to Nova Scotia and probably escaped from cultivation. It is scattered throughout but is abundant locally in fields and meadows.

Chrysanthemum leucanthemum
Ox-eye Daisy

The appearance of daisies marks the end of spring and the beginning of summer. The showy flowers with the long white rays are distinctive and known to all. Ox-eye Daisies are common throughout Nova Scotia and one of the best-known flowers of our fields and meadows.

Cornus canadensis
Bunchberry

The Bunchberry is easy to recognize because of the whorl of leaves near the top of its stem and the four showy white bracts that surround its small and relatively insignificant flower. The berries, which form in bunches, are red and mealy. Bunchberry grows in beds of low plants, less than 10 cm tall, which become con-spicuous in early June in barrens and mature bogs and along the edges of woodlands. Bunchberry is common in coniferous woods and in blueberry fields.

Galium palustre
Marsh-bedstraw

The tiny white flowers of the Bedstraw soon dot the grasses in any low place in mid-June. Its flowers have four petals and its leaves are in whorls. The Marsh-bedstraw is very common throughout Nova Scotia in meadows and along streams.

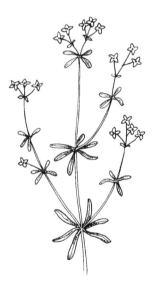

Gnaphalium uliginosum
Low Cudweed

Low Cudweed is an annual plant beginning to flower in June. The whole plant is usually whitish-woolly, and the flowers are brownish. This low plant is common everywhere in poorly drained soil in gardens and fields.

Malva moschata
Musk Mallow

This plant forms clumps with conspicuous pink or white flowers. The petals of Musk Mallow flowers are very delicate in texture and the column of numerous stamens, which surround the female portion of the flower, is a distinguishing characteristic. Several other species bloom later in the summer. Musk Mallow occurs locally throughout Nova Scotia in gardens but more often in fields or along roadsides.

Menyanthes trifoliata
Buckbean

Buckbean is a stout smooth plant about 40 cm tall that grows in bogs or stagnant pools, usually with its base covered by water. Its thick leaves, with their three leaflets, and its very unusual white flowers are both distinctive, the upper surface of the flower petals being covered with hair. It is common from Kings and Cumberland counties to Cape Breton but rare in the southwestern counties.

Oxalis montana
Wood-sorrel

Wood-sorrel is a low plant, about 10 cm tall. Its three leaflets per leaf make it easy to identify. Wood-sorrel flowers are white, but veined with pink. It is common in moist woods, along ravines, and in wooded swamps throughout Nova Scotia.

Plantago lanceolata
Narrow-leaved Plantain

The spikes of Narrow-leaved Plantain's greenish-white flowers are short, almost cone-shaped, and sit at the top of slender stalks. The leaves are long and narrow and grow quite erect. It is common throughout the province in old fields. Unlike the Broad-leaved Plantain, it is rarely found around buildings.

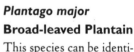

Plantago major
Broad-leaved Plantain

This species can be identified by the broad leaves which grow flat upon the ground. Its tall narrow spikes of insignificant greenish-white flowers begin to develop by the middle of June. Broad-leaved Plantain is very common in lawns, gardens, and dooryards.

fruit

Sanicula marilandica
Black Snakeroot

Black Snakeroot flowers are greenish-white and arranged in inconspicuous umbels. The leaves are palmately divided; the fruits are bristly, making them fairly distinctive. This species is relatively common in rich woods and intervales throughout the province.

Spergula arvensis
Spurrey

This plant is an annual growing up to 30 cm tall. A member of the Chickweed Family, its white flowers are small and numerous with unlobed petals. Its leaves are very narrow, thread-like, and occur in whorls. Spurrey is common in grain fields and gardens.

Non-Woody (Herbaceous) Plants

DICOTS
Regular flowers
Yellow flowers

Chelidonium majus
Celandine

Celandine may be a metre or so tall with lobed leaves. Its flower has two sepals and four yellow petals. A main identifying feature is the bright saffron-coloured juice that appears when any part of the plant is broken. Celandine flowers from late June onward. You can find it scattered in the southwestern region of the province and eastward to Halifax.

Erysimum cheiranthoides
Wormseed Mustard

The tiny yellow flowers of Wormseed Mustard open at the top of the plant while the older ones form seed-pods. The flowers have four tiny petals, typical of this plant family, and the pods diverge horizontally and then grow erect. Wormseed Mustard is common around farmyards and in gardens throughout the province. It flowers from June to September.

Hieracium floribundum
King-devil

King-devil is a low plant, about 30 cm tall, common in old fields and along roadsides. Later in the summer, entire fields may be yellow with it. The flowers are showy with numerous rays. It is distinguished by having a number of flower-heads per stem and frequent stolons (runners). King-devil is common in most parts of Nova Scotia.

Hieracium piloselloides
Yellow Hawkweed

The common type of Yellow Hawkweed, without stolons, is included here, although various types may be present. As with other species of Hawkweed, it begins to flower in June and its flowers are still common in mid-summer. You can find Yellow Hawkweed throughout Nova Scotia.

Hypochoeris radicata
Cat's-ear

The plant is about 30 cm tall and in places forms a continuous line along the road-shoulder. It resembles the Fall Dandelion but is a much more rugged plant with abundant stiff hairs. Cat's-ear has become common in Yarmouth County and is rapidly spreading eastward along roadsides.

Leontodon autumnalis
Fall Dandelion, August-flower

The lobed leaves of the Fall Dandelion originate at the base of the plant and the slender branched stems have showy yellow flowers at their tips. Although this species is usually associated with the summer and fall, it may begin to flower by the middle of June. It is common throughout the province, especially on lawns, in fields, and along roadsides after the grass has been cut.

Oenothera perennis
Small Sundrops

The yellow flowers of Small Sundrops have four large petals that grow from the axils of the leaves. The young flowering shoots nod at their tips. The plants can usually be found scattered in old fields and along roadsides throughout the province.

Oenothera tetragona
Sundrops

Sundrops are slender plants with yellow flowers. In this species the young flowering tip is not nodding. The plant is slightly larger but, otherwise, much like Small Sundrops and found in similar habitats. It tends to be more common in the southern part of the province.

Ranunculus acris
Tall Buttercup

This is the familiar buttercup of fields and meadows. The lower leaves are cut, but not divided, into stalked leaflets. The bright yellow flowers, with many carpels and stamens, are typical of all the buttercups. All of our species have an acrid taste.

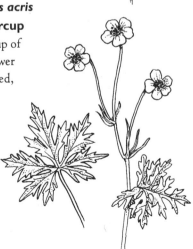

Ranunculus recurvatus
Woodland Buttercup

This is one of our woodland buttercups. Its leaves are divided into three wide lobes and the yellow flowers are small, or tiny on early plants. You can find it on wooded hillsides and intervales from Digby and Cumberland counties to northern Cape Breton; it is absent in the southwestern counties and along the Atlantic coast.

Ranunculus repens
Creeping Buttercup

The Creeping Buttercup, with its yellow flowers, is very similar to the Tall Buttercup, but it more often creeps and has lower leaves that are deeply divided with stalked leaflets. It usually, but not always, has creeping basal branches and may form tangles along ditches and in wet hollows throughout the province.

Senecio vulgaris
Common
Groundsel

Common Groundsel begins to flower early in June and continues until late autumn. Rays are absent, so the golden-yellow flower is not showy. This plant is a member of the Asteraceae, as are Cat's-ear, Fall Dandelion, King-devil, and Yellow Hawkweed. This genus has only one row of long bracts surrounding the flower head. Common Groundsel, a common annual, is locally well-established in waste places, in gardens, and around many of the fishing villages. It is widespread.

Tragopogon
pratensis
Goat's-beard

Goat's-beard is a tall unbranched plant that grows over 50 cm tall with long leaves and a deep tap-root. The yellow flowers and the head of seeds are very much like those of a dandelion, but on a larger scale. It begins to flower by the middle of June. It is common in waste places and is spreading out into grasslands in many areas of the province.

Non-Woody (Herbaceous) Plants

DICOTS
Regular flowers
Yellowish-green flowers

Alchemilla xanthochlora
Lady's-mantle

Lady's-mantle tends to grow in patches, from 10 to 20 cm tall. Its yellowish-green flowers are small with no petals, but with four sepals alternating with four tiny bractlets. It continues to flower throughout the summer. Lady's-mantle is common in southwestern Nova Scotia, where it is abundant and aggressive near the coast, although it is less abundant inland.

Euphorbia cyparissias
Cypress Spurge

Cypress Spurge resembles small fir trees growing about 20 cm tall. Its yellowish or greenish flowers are small and insignificant, but they are surrounded by two yellowish bracts which are conspicuous. It can be found scattered as an escape from cultivation, often around old cemeteries, and occasionally along roadsides and in fields.

Non-Woody (Herbaceous) Plants

DICOTS
Regular flowers
Green flowers

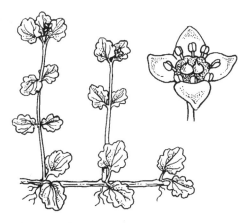

Chrysosplenium americanum
Northern Saxifrage

The Northern Saxifrage is a small prostrate plant which forms mats in hollows in wet woods, around springs, or along trickling rills. The green flowers are very small and inconspicuous. They have no petals but do have four to eight stamens. Common throughout the northern section of the province, Northern Saxifrage tends to be absent in Yarmouth County and is not found in acidic soils.

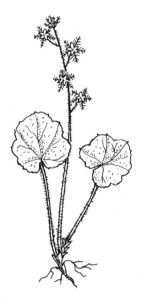

Mitella nuda
Miterwort

This delicate plant is only about 10 cm tall with light-coloured greenish flowers. The finely divided, filamentous petals are the conspicuous part of the plant. Miterwort is common in wooded swamps and mossy woods from Annapolis County to northern Cape Breton, rare in Yarmouth County, and absent on the Atlantic side of the province.

Non-Woody (Herbaceous) Plants

DICOTS
Regular flowers
Blue flowers

Solanum dulcamara
Bittersweet

Bittersweet is a stiff vine with irregularly lobed leaves. The flowers, which resemble those of potato or tomato, are blue in colour and produce green berries, which later turn bright red. It is our only spring-flowering vine. It is scattered throughout Nova Scotia.

Symphytum officinale
Common Comfrey

Common Comfrey is a coarse, old-fashioned garden plant, found scattered around houses or adjacent roadsides. The flowers are tubular and vary in colour from a light blue to a creamy white. The plants are rough and hairy; they tend to grow in patches and up to a metre tall. Scattered throughout the province, it tends to be more common in Pictou and Kings counties.

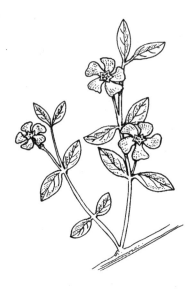

Vinca minor
Myrtle, Periwinkle

Myrtle is a trailing plant grown mostly as a ground cover. Its thick leaves are evergreen and its blue flowers are scattered. The leaves are opposite, with the flower found in the axil of only one leaf of the pair. The corolla is deeply five-lobed. It is occasionally cultivated and persists along roadsides or in old cemeteries; so it is most common around established communities.

Non-Woody (Herbaceous) Plants

DICOTS
Regular flowers
Orange flowers

Hieracium aurantiacum
**Orange Hawkweed,
Devil's Paint-brush**

Hawkweeds are common in Nova Scotia and a number of species are present. This is the only one with bright orange flowers. Devil's Paint-brush is a rather rough plant, about 10 cm tall, with numerous flower heads to a stalk. It may be found scattered throughout, but tends to be more common in the central regions of Nova Scotia.

Non-Woody (Herbaceous) Plants

DICOTS
Regular flowers
Pinkish, red, or purple flowers

Geranium robertianum
Herb-Robert

The deeply lobed or divided leaves and small pinkish flowers of Herb-Robert will serve to identify it. It is common from Digby County to northern Cape Breton, growing in rocky woods, on talus slopes, and in cool ravines. It is also some-times found in the rocky areas behind sea-beaches.

Hesperis matronalis
Rocket, Dame's Violet

Rocket is an old-fashioned garden plant, growing to over a metre tall, and usually occurring in masses with pale purple or whitish flowers that have four petals. It was formerly widely grown in gardens but persists now in patches along roadsides or in waste places.

Rumex acetosa
Garden-sorrel

Garden-sorrel is conspicuous in June when the
plants become nearly a metre tall. It is much
larger than Sheep-sorrel and has leaves of
a different outline. The reddish or
greenish flowers are very tiny, each one
producing a single seed. It is rapidly
spreading around dwellings and in old
fields, where patches of it may be seen. It
is common in the Annapolis Valley and
along the South Shore, but scattered
throughout.

Spergularia rubra
Sand Spurrey

Sand Spurrey is a tiny chickweed
less than 10 cm tall. The leaves are
opposite and the flowers are pink.
However, its petals are not lobed at
the tip, thus they are different from
those of many of the chickweeds. Sand
Spurrey is found as a scattered introduc-
tion throughout Nova Scotia on sandy or
gravelly soils around farmyards and in
waste places.

Index

The page that contains the illustration of the flower is shown in **boldface** type.

NOTES

NOTES